CHRISTIAN FOUNDATIONS

Plumbline Adult Bible Teaching Series, Book 1

GWEN THORNTON

April 2022
ISBN: 978-1-64457-274-0

Rise UP Publications
644 Shrewsbury Commons Ave
Ste 249
Shrewsbury PA 17361
United States of America
www.riseUPpublications.com
Phone: 866-846-5123

I am a teacher
because I am a lifelong student
that is in love with this awesome author
of this book called the Bible.

TABLE OF CONTENTS

FOREWORD

I was 'that kid' that every teacher dreaded. Born and raised in Wilmington, Delaware, I was an angry and lost teenager. I struggled in school and rebelled in church.

In 1982 gave my life to Jesus Christ. After my salvation, I began serving in children's ministry, where my gift to teach grew.

In my 35+ years of teaching, I have taught students in all age categories. God gifted me with the ability to break down His Word so that children could understand.

As I grew, so did the gift to teach. I found that God could use my past experiences and translate them into teachable moments for all ages and that God would also use them to reach those who didn't fit into the perfect "church mold."

Throughout the years I purchased curriculum from various sources. Some were good, but most were just okay. I found myself having to rewrite most of the material, and I became increasingly frustrated.

That demand forced me to seek the heart of God for all of my lesson planning. I understood then, as I do now, that the sole key to great lesson planning is seeking the heart of God. The Great Teacher, The Holy Spirit, would show me creative ways to break down His Word by using object lessons, props, skits, stories, food, and more.

I personally find great joy in breaking down the Word in simple ways so that any student can retain it. My curriculum has now expanded from children and youth, to women's and adult Bible studies. The Holy Spirit's guidance prevails in directing me.

As the ministry grew, I needed to supply new teachers with teaching materials. Because I couldn't duplicate myself, I had to re-write my lessons for new teachers to use. (It is much easier to write lessons for your personal use, but much more challenging to write lessons for others to teach.)

It was never my intention to write curriculum for others to use. I merely filled a need and recognized that the lessons were beneficial in laying the foundations of faith in the life of believers.

I have now tallied about five years of comprehensive lessons for multiple ages. The study of the Word of God has been a gift to me. Great teachers of faith sowed into me the 'love' of the Word. For them, I am deeply grateful.

The Word kept me from being deceived by various winds of doctrine and has been my rock through some very difficult times. Perhaps that is why I am especially passionate about helping children and new believers build solid foundations in Christ.

In my role as a wife, mother, grandmother and pastor, I know the power of this curriculum in both the life of the individual and in the life of a local church.

I am humbled and honored that you are using this curriculum to lay the foundations of faith in your own life and/or in the life of those God has entrusted for you to teach. I pray you find it easy to understand and use. It is my prayer that you, too, will discover the riches and rewards of walking with our Lord and Savior, Jesus Christ.

—*Gwen Thornton*

LESSON # 1: THE TRINITY

If you were to fill in a "Hello my name is" sticker and write your name on it, is that the only name you go by?

How many other names do you go by besides your actual name? For example: Teacher, sister, Pastor, Friend, Grandparent, Grandchild, etc.…

Write down the names below:

1.
2.
3.
4.
5.

Does this mean that you are more than one person? Of course not!

In the same way, God is one God. Yet, His identity is defined through different names and more specifically, three persons:

- God—the Father
- God—the Son
- God—the Holy Spirit

Example: Water (H20)

- a liquid form—water
- a solid form—ice
- a gas form—steam

It remains H2O no matter what form it takes.

In the same manner as water, God is God whether He is in the person of God the Father, God the Son, or God the Holy Spirit. He is still one God, just as the substance we know as water is still H2O.

Father–Son–Holy Spirit

- **Three** distinct persons yet **one** God!
- Trinity—Three in One
- God has three distinct roles:
    1. **Son** (Jesus)—is the Word made flesh (the body)
    2. **Holy Spirit**—Life of God (Power of God)
    3. **Father**—Mind, Will, and Emotions

Old Testament Example Of Three Different Roles Of God During Creation

- **God the Father**
    - **Genesis 1:1** (NASB)—*In the beginning* ***God created*** *the heavens and the earth.*
    - See God the Father created
- **God the Holy Spirit**
    - **Genesis 1:2** (NASB)—*The earth was formless and void, and darkness was over the surface of the deep, and the* ***Spirit of God was moving over*** *the surface of the waters.*
    - See God the Spirit of God moving
- **God the Son**
    - **Genesis 1:3** (NASB) —*Then God* ***said****, "Let there be light"; and there was light.*
    - Spoke the Word (Jesus)

New Testament Example Of Three Different Roles Of God

- Jesus being water baptized

Matthew 3:13-17 (NASB)—*Then Jesus arrived from Galilee at the Jordan coming to John, to be baptized by him. But John tried to prevent Him, saying, "I have need to be baptized by You, and do You come to me?" But Jesus answering said to him, "Permit it at this time; for in this way it is fitting for us to fulfill all righteousness." Then he permitted Him. After being baptized, Jesus came up immediately from the water; and behold, the heavens were opened, and he saw the Spirit of God descending as a dove and lighting on Him, and behold, a voice out of the heavens said, "This is My beloved Son, in whom I am well-pleased."*

- God the **Father** spoke, God the **Holy Spirit** descended, and God the **Son** (Jesus) was in the flesh.

God Makes Man In His Image

Genesis 1:26 (NASB)—*Then God said, "**Let Us** make man in **Our image**, according to **Our likeness**; and let them rule over the fish of the sea and over the birds of the sky and over the cattle and over all the earth, and over every creeping thing that creeps on the earth."*

- Us? Our? Who is He talking about?
  - Father, Son, and Holy Spirit—three in One (He is speaking to Himself)
- Let Us make man in **Our image** according to **Our likeness** and let them rule!
  - He differentiates between Image and Likeness

Example: A man and woman have a baby. The baby is made in their image and may look like one parent or the other, but they may not grow up to be like either one of them.

We Are A Three-Part Being Like God

We are a spirit, live in a body, and possess a soul:

1. **Body**—our flesh
2. **Soul**—mind, will, and emotions (heart) – thinking, feeling, and purpose
3. **Spirit**—life (God breathed life into man)

Example: Crack open an egg—there are three parts. A shell, an egg white, and a yoke—body, soul & spirit. This is how God created us in three parts, just like Him.

New Testament Scripture

I Thes. 5:23 (NASB)—*Now may the God of peace Himself sanctify you entirely; and may your spirit and soul and body be preserved complete without blame at the coming of our Lord Jesus Christ.*

John 1:1-3 (NASB)—*In the beginning was the Word, and the Word was with God. He was in the beginning with God. All things came into being by Him, and apart from Him nothing came into being that has come into being.*

Made In His Likeness

- **God made man in His likeness**—His personality (perfect love, integrity, righteousness, peace, joy, etc.)
- **Genesis 2:7** (NASB)—*Then the Lord God formed man of dust from the ground, and breathed into his nostrils the breath of life; and man became a living being.*
- **God breathed** into man the breath of life (Genesis 2:7)
  - Man became a living being—a three-part being like God
  - Man is different from animals and angels.
- We were created to **look like** Him and **ACT like** Him (image and likeness)

God Made Man To Rule

Genesis 1:28 (NASB)—*God blessed them; and God said to them, "Be fruitful and multiply, and fill the earth, and subdue it; and rule over the fish of the sea and over the birds of the sky and over every living thing that moves on the earth."*

God created the earth and mankind to take dominion, rule, and self-govern.

- We were created to rule the earth and ourselves
- Our spirit was created to rule our soul and body (*spirit in charge*)
- Spirit of man
  - Knowing
  - Seeing
  - Full of Power
- God wanted us to be **like** Him!

Summarize

- Made in His Image (look like God—spirit, soul, and body)
- Made in His Likeness (act like God)
- Made to self-rule (the spirit to rule the body and soul)

Genesis 2:16-17 (NASB)— *The Lord God commanded the man, saying, "From any tree of the garden you may eat freely; but from the tree of the knowledge of good and evil you shall not eat, for in the day that you eat from it you will surely die."*

Genesis 3:1-7 (NASB)—*Now the serpent was more crafty than any beast of the field which the Lord God had made. And he said to the woman, "Indeed, has God said, 'You shall not eat from any tree of the garden?" The woman said to the serpent, "From the fruit of the trees of the garden we may eat; but from the fruit of the tree which is in the middle of the garden, God has said, 'You shall not eat from it or touch it, or you will die.'" The serpent said to the woman, "You surely will not die! For God knows that in the day you eat from it your eyes will be opened, and you will be like God, knowing good and evil." When the woman saw that the tree was good for food, and that it was a delight to the eyes, and that the tree was desirable to make one wise, she took from its fruit and ate; and she gave also to her husband with her, and he ate. Then the eyes of both of them were opened, and they knew that they were naked; and they sewed fig leaves together and made themselves loin coverings.*

- If you **eat of the tree** of the knowledge of good and evil, **you will die**
- The temptation and the fall of man (Gen 3:1-7) Satan tempts them and deceives them, and they eat from the tree.
- Vs. 7—What happened? Their eyes were opened, to what? (their spiritual eyes were opened to evil—the god of this world Satan entered in)
- Like a villain who hatches an evil plan and they just got captured!
- Thru deception, **the enemy caused man to fall into sin so he could steal his kingdom** – mankind lost his ability **to rule himself** and **the earth**.
- They knew they were naked or taken over!
- They lost their knowing, seeing, and the power to do.
- The devil deceived them into believing that God was withholding something good from them, but in reality, God did not want them to know evil.

- They immediately felt the loss of His presence and saw evil and felt evil for the first time.
    - Vs. 8—they hid themselves (shame)
    - Vs. 10—fear
    - Vs. 11—who told you that you were naked (uncovered)
    - Vs. 12—blame
    - Vs. 21—first murder

They Lost The "Likeness" Of God

- sin entered man
- Sin ruled their lives
- They were no longer **"like"** God
- Their soul—mind, will, and emotions ruled them instead of their spirit man.
- Their spirit was separated from the Spirit of God
- No power, no authority, full of fear, guilt, shame, anger, pain, sickness, death etc.

God Never Wanted Them To Know Evil (Genesis 3:22)

- He wanted them to know **"goodness of God"** all their lives.
- If they had eaten of the tree of life after their spiritual death, they would have lived forever only knowing **good and evil without a savior!**
- God kicked them out of the garden and put an angel in front of the tree of life to guard it.
- God promised to send them a deliverer/savior from the mess they created for themselves and their children.

Man Needs A Hero

He sent a savior to restore man back to **his original place**—as a spirit-led individual.

- We were created for our spirit to rule our soul and our body.
- But when man sinned, his spirit was disconnected from God, and his soul was left to rule his being.

Example: Vacuum cleaner hose; if it gets disconnected from the canister, it loses power. It still has electricity but no suction. That is what happened to mankind when they sinned!

Redemption

When we get **born again**—we come full circle.

- Restores our position with God
- Our **spirit is made alive, and power is restored**. We now have the ability to overcome the enemy and to rule again (**when submitted to God,** we can now receive His direction, His wisdom, His character, and His nature). We are given back our powers!
- Reconnected to the "canister" (God) and functioning the way we were created.
- Our **soul** (mind, will and emotions)
    - Wholeness
    - It changes where our soul will spend eternity (heaven instead of hell)
- Our **bodies**—we will receive a new heavenly body
- The only thing that does not get restored is that man still knows good and evil, and our bodies will eventually die or be resurrected.
- Mankind will always battle the enemy as long as we live on this earth, but as children of God we have the power, authority, and the tools to win!

Mankind was created in God's "image and after His likeness". We were created to live spirit-led lives in close relationship to God. When man sinned, he yielded his authority to Satan (god of this world's systems). God however, set the boundaries and announced that Satan will only have authority to "bruise our heels," but we will "bruise his head". This basically means that Satan, the "god of this world", will always try to affect your walk with God.

Once you are "born again, you regain your authority over the "god of this world" and regain the ability to lead a Spirit led life in close relationship to God. The Spirit led individual will overcome the wicked one.

God never wanted us to be without Him. As a born-again believer, we must understand that we still have to take the time to learn God's ways, renew our minds, and develop our character to resist the temptations of the "god of this world". Learning to be led by the Holy Spirit is what sets the born-again believer apart from those who do not know Christ.

Closing

God is a three-part being, and we were made like God as a three-part being (body, soul and spirit)

Say this aloud: *I am a spirit, I live in a body and I possess my soul!*

LESSON # 1: HOMEWORK

Homework Assignment

Read the article below and look up the following scriptures in the Bible on the "Trinity" (https://bible.org/node/15556)

The Trinity

God is a trinity (*three in one*) of persons: the Father, the Son, and the Holy Spirit. The Father is not the same person as the Son; the Son is not the same person as the Holy Spirit; and the Holy Spirit is not the same person as Father. They are not three gods and not three beings. They are three distinct persons; yet, they are all the one God. Each has a will, can speak, can love, etc., and these are demonstrations of personhood. They are in absolute perfect harmony consisting of one substance. They are coeternal, coequal, and co-powerful. If any one of the three were removed, there would be no God.

Jesus, the Son, is one person with two natures: Divine and Human. This is called the Hypostatic Union. The Holy Spirit is also divine in nature and is self aware, the third person of the Trinity.

A further point of clarification is that God is not one person, the Father, with Jesus as a creation and the Holy Spirit as a force (Jehovah's Witnesses). Neither is He one person who took three consecutive forms, i.e., the Father, became the Son, who became the Holy Spirit. Nor is God the divine nature of the Son (where Jesus had a human nature perceived as the Son and a divine nature perceived as the Father (Oneness theology). Nor is the Trinity an office held by three separate Gods (Mormonism).

The word "person" is used to describe the three members of the Godhead because the word "person" is appropriate. A person is self-aware, can speak, love, hate, say "you," "yours," "me," "mine," etc. Each of the three persons in the Trinity demonstrates these qualities.

The chart below should help you to see how the doctrine of the Trinity is systematically derived from Scripture. The list is not exhaustive, only illustrative.

The first step is to establish the biblical doctrine that there is only one God. Then, you find that each of the persons is called God, each creates, each was involved in Jesus' resurrection, each indwells, etc. Therefore, God is one, but the one God is in three simultaneous persons. Please note that the idea of a composite unity is not a foreign concept to the Bible; after all, man and wife are said to be one flesh. The idea of a composite unity of persons is spoken of by God in Genesis (Genesis 2:24).

Scripture Look Up

Look up the following scriptures and see if you can identify the three persons in the godhead. They are three distinct persons; yet, they are all the one God.

I Corinthians 8:6	John 10:30	1 John 5:7-8
2 Corinthians 3:17	Luke 1:35	1 Peter 1:1-2
2 Corinthians 13:14	Matthew 1:23	2 Corinthians 1:21-22
Colossians 2:9	Matthew 28:19	1 Corinthians 12:4-6
Isaiah 9:6	Matthew 3:16-17	Ephesians 4:4-6
Isaiah 9:6	John 14:16-17	John 14:9-11
Isaiah 44:6	Romans 14:17-18	John 10:30-36
John 1:14	Luke 3:21-22	

LESSON # 2: FORBIDDEN FRUIT

Supplies: A basket of Granny Smith Apples (or any apples that are all one color); One Macintosh apple (1/2 green & ½ red), and 1 rotten apple.

Have three apples on display: one green, one mixed (red and green – Macintosh & Granny Smith), and one rotten.

Pick up the rotten apple and ask: Would anyone like to eat this apple?

There is not much difference between the two good apples (*Granny Smith & Macintosh*)—one was forbidden, one was not! Use them as you illustrate your lesson.

Show them the Macintosh apple and the Granny Smith (green apple) – ask if they look good to eat.

(Green ones represent the fruit from the tree of life and the other the fruit from the tree of the knowledge of good and evil – green/red)

Refer back to the apples throughout your lesson.

The Creation Of Man And Woman

Genesis 2:1-8 (NASB)—*Thus the heavens and the earth were completed, and all their hosts. By the seventh day God completed His work which He had done, and He rested on the seventh day from all His work which He had done. Then God blessed the seventh day and sanctified it, because in it He rested from all His work which God had created and made.*

This is the account of the heavens and the earth when they were created, in the day that the LORD God made earth and heaven. Now no shrub of the field was yet in the earth, and no plant of the field had yet sprouted, for the LORD God had not sent rain upon the earth, and there was no man to cultivate the ground. But a mist used to rise from the earth and water the whole surface of the ground. Then the LORD God formed man of dust from the ground, and breathed into his nostrils the breath of life; and man became a living being. The LORD God planted a garden toward the east, in Eden; and there He placed the man whom He had formed.

There Were Two Trees In The Garden

Genesis 2:9-17 (NASB)—*Out of the ground the LORD God caused to grow every tree that is pleasing to the sight and good for food; the tree of life also in the midst of the garden, and the tree of the knowledge of good and evil.*

Then the LORD God took the man and put him into the Garden of Eden to cultivate it and keep it. The LORD God commanded the man, saying, "From any tree of the garden you may eat freely; but from the tree of the knowledge of good and evil you shall not eat, for in the day that you eat from it you will surely die."

- **Tree of Life**
    - They could eat as much as they wanted (*show a green apple*)
    - It kept them alive physically
- **Tree of the knowledge of good and evil**
    - good and evil (*2 distinct things—one fruit, show the red & green apple—the Macintosh*)
    - I can understand why they were not to eat of the evil part, but why not the good? *We will find out in a little bit....*

The Fall Of Man

Genesis 3:1-7 (NASB)—*Now the serpent (Hebrew means: shining one) was craftier than any beast of the field which the Lord God had made. And he said to the woman, "Indeed, has God said, 'You shall not eat from any tree of the garden'?" The woman said to the serpent, "From the fruit of the trees of the garden we may eat; but from the fruit of the tree which is in the middle of the garden, God has said, 'You shall not eat from it or touch it, or you will die.'" The serpent said to the woman, "You surely will not die! For God knows that in the day you eat from it your eyes will be opened, and you will be like God, knowing good and evil." When the woman saw that the tree was good for food, and that it was a delight to the eyes, and that the tree was desirable to make one wise, she took from its fruit and ate; and she gave also to her husband with her, and he ate. Then the eyes of both of them were opened, and they knew that they were naked; and they sewed fig leaves together and made themselves loin coverings.*

Let's Go back and dissect these two passages and see what was really said!

God Said...

Genesis 2:16-17 (NASB)—*The LORD God commanded the man, saying, "From any tree of the garden you may eat freely; but from the tree of the knowledge of good and evil you shall not eat, for in the day that you eat from it you will surely die."*

The Serpent (The Devil) Said...

Genesis 3:1 (NASB)—*And he said to the woman, "Indeed, has God said, 'You shall not eat from any tree of the garden?'"*

- Note: This is the first question mark in the Bible!

Eve (The Woman) Said...

Genesis 3:2-3 (NASB)—*The woman said to the serpent, "From the fruit of the trees of the garden we may eat; but from the fruit of the tree which is in the middle of the garden, God has said, 'You shall not eat from it or touch it (add on by Eve), or you will die.*

The Serpent (The Devil)Said...

Genesis 3:4-5 (NASB)—*The serpent said to the woman, "You surely will not die! For God knows that in the day you eat from it your eyes will be opened, and you will be like God, knowing good and evil."*

Eve (The Woman) Said...

Genesis 3:6 (NASB)—*When the woman saw that the tree was good for food, and that it was a delight to the eyes, and that the tree was desirable to make one wise, she took from its fruit and ate; and she gave also to her husband with her, and he ate.*

Genesis 3:7 (NASB)—*Then the eyes (singular) of both of them were opened, and they knew that they were naked; and they sewed fig leaves together and made themselves loin coverings.*

What Happened?

The **Serpent** promised Adam and Eve that their **eyes** would "**be opened**" if they ate of the fruit of the tree of **knowledge of good and evil**.

Weren't their eyes already open? Let's dig a little deeper…

Who is this Serpent?

- Lucifer/Satan - Hebrew meaning (*light bearer, light bringer—shining one*)

What Eyes?

- In Hebrew, it can be translated as "**knowledge**".
- Hebrew word for "eyes" is not plural but **singular**.
- What the Serpent actually told Adam and Eve was that their "**eye" (singular) would be broadened by knowledge**.
- The "eye" that Scripture wants us to consider is not the physical organ of sight but the **eye of the mind or the soul**.

Opened To What?

- Opened can be translated as "**broadened.**"
- What the Serpent promised Adam and Eve was that knowledge would be broadened if they ate of the forbidden fruit. (*spiritually enlightened*)
- The Devil has had mankind on a **spiritual quest** ever since, trying to deceive or convince mankind that "he" is the one who leads us into **enlightenment or spiritual oneness!**

Note: This singular "eye" is called the "third eye" of clairvoyance in the Hindu religion, the eye of Osiris in Egypt, and the All-Seeing Eye in Freemasonry.

The Two Trees

Tree of Life

- They could eat as much as they wanted, it kept them alive physically. How do I know?

- Because God set an angel to guard it and keep them from eating it after they sinned so that they couldn't eat it and live forever. He didn't want them to live forever knowing good and evil.

Genesis 3:22 (NASB)—*Then the LORD God said, "Behold, the man has become like one of Us, knowing good and evil; and now, he might stretch out his hand, and take also from the tree of life, and eat, and live forever" therefore the LORD God sent him out from the garden of Eden, to cultivate the ground from which he was taken. So He drove the man out; and at the east of the garden of Eden He stationed the cherubim and the flaming sword which turned every direction to guard the way to the tree of life.*

Tree of the Knowledge of Good and Evil

- We think **good is the opposite side of evil**, but God didn't want them to eat of the tree that had **either good or evil**. Why?
- It isn't a ying/yang (*equal parts of good and evil*) tree, then again maybe it is?
- The good that is in you is evil by nature?
- Have you ever heard the Expression the lesser of two evils? People will say well I had to choose the lesser of two evils? What does that mean?
- This good is the lesser of two evils but it is still evil! (*disguised to deceive us into thinking it is okay but it is really still evil that leads to death*)

Illustration: Macintosh apple—Notice the apple from the good and evil is desirable. If it was only evil (rotten) they wouldn't have been tempted! The Devil had to disguise the evil by making it look "good".

It is like the poison apple from the Snow White movie, it looked good but it was full of poison!

Rotten apple—if it had looked rotten/evil they wouldn't have eaten it.

What Is "Good"?

Something pleasant, agreeable to the **senses** (soul–mind, will, and emotions)

- Pleasures (make us "feel" good)
- Our soul takes pleasure in doing good and God things – what is the difference? God things please God and lead to life!
- There are a lot of "good things" that make us feel "good", but do not please God.

- There are a ton of "good groups", "good deeds", "good intentions" and "good people"
- They can separate us from God (His will and His plan)
- The result of this "good" caused death
- A <u>good</u> which is the enemy of God's perfect will and perfect plan.
- It was an understanding of good that <u>seemed right to man,</u> but a good which in the end was capable of bringing destruction and misery. It would cause man to try to do good works apart from God's leadership and direction.

Note: Good things are not always God things, but God things are always good!

How Do We Know If Something Is Of God Or "Good"?

It causes us to:

- Question God and His Word?
- Disobey God?
- Separate us from God?
- Replace Him?

2 Corinthians 6:14 (NASB 1995)—*Do not be bound together with unbelievers; for what partnership have righteousness and lawlessness, or what fellowship has light with darkness? Good says, "I desire it so it doesn't matter if it is sin!"*

Example: God vs. good—Sex is God-ordained, but outside of marriage between a man and a woman it is "good" but leads to death!

The Devil's goal is not to just get you to fall into sin; he wants you to live your life without God! Live the "good" life and make you think you are alright with God and end up in hell…the greatest deception ever!

Evil "Ra" In Hebrew

- He gained **entrance** when they ate of the fruit
- Remember "RA" was the Egyptian god (the god of the Illuminati today)
- The shining one, Light bearer, light bringer, illumination
- Evil illustration—we don't need an illustration to explain evil, do we? Even ungodly people know what evil is.

The Temptation Of Sin

- She looked on it—gazed at it (eyes are the window "opening" of the soul)
- She turned to it
- A voice called to Eve
- She talked with the enemy, and he convinced her that you don't need God. He is trying to keep you from being "wise".
- The enemy convinced her that they would **not** die, and if you eat of it, you will have knowledge and be like God, knowing good and evil!
- For one brief moment, they actually thought what the serpent was telling them could be true.
- Their hearts were lifted up in pride—they could be wise like God—they could be "their own god"
- Independence, Rebellion (misplaced authority) had entered the heart of man. (self-governing—by myself)

The Plot Of The Enemy

The Plot of the Enemy was to get mankind to sin against God *(he uses the same old tricks today)*

- The Devil Questioned what God said! (*Here we find the first question mark in the Bible—drops that seed into her mind*)
- Eve answers and adds to what God said (*or touch it*)
- You surely shall not die (*tells her that there will be no consequence*)
- The Devil convinces her that God just doesn't want her to know what <u>He knows</u> (*God is selfish—withholding something good from them)*
- She **saw that is was good** for food, and that it was a **delight to the eyes**, and that the tree was **desirable** to make **one wise**—she ate it!
- God created mankind with free will, the freedom to choose.

First, the Devil **spoke** deception to her, then he **showed** it to her and **deceived** her into believing she was missing out on something and that there would be no consequences!

Her response—She listened, looked, gazed, desired, and gave in, hoping to get wise!

The Results Of Sin

Illustration: Candle—light a candle and then blow it out (the wick is still intact)

Gen 2:16-17 (NASB)—*The LORD God commanded the man, saying, "From any tree of the garden you may eat freely; but from the tree of the knowledge of good and evil you shall not eat, for in the day that you eat from it you will surely die."*

- God said, if you eat of the tree of the knowledge of good and evil you will die, they ate of the fruit, and they died, not physically, but they became spiritually separated from God.
- The death process began in their physical bodies, and time began as we know it.

What Happened To Them When They Ate The Forbidden Fruit Of The Knowledge Of Good And Evil? Did They Die?

When Adam and Eve made their decision to disobey their Heavenly Father, Eve reached out her hand and took of the forbidden fruit, ate it, and gave it to Adam who was standing beside her, and he ate it, too. (Genesis 3:6)

- They immediately felt **the loss of His presence** and **saw and felt evil for the first time**. (*As soon as they had disobeyed God's command they realized that, like little children who had strayed too far from their parent's side, they were lost from God's presence)*
- The glorious light of the **knowledge of God** that had illuminated their souls suddenly **left them**.
- They were stripped of the royal power and authority that God had given them on the day that they were created. Example: Like superman losing his power!
- Their eyes **lost the ability to see into the heavenly realms**
- They were **no longer able to see God and His holy angels**
- All the **joy and laughter that they enjoyed left their hearts**
- Instead of becoming wise, they **lost their mental capacity and became dull**
- The **knowledge of evil had entered their hearts** producing fear, worry and confusion and every wicked thing *(I picture it like a being flooded in their minds with bad thoughts and feelings, like a bad nightmare)*
- This death also made them want to **hide from God** instead of enjoying His presence.

- They were **overcome with guilt, misery and shame** they hid themselves among the trees hoping that their heavenly Father would not discover what they had done.
- This death had also caused **a knowledge of good**—a good which was the enemy of God's perfect will and God's perfect plan. It was an understanding of good that seemed right to man, but a good which in the end was capable of bringing destruction and misery. It would cause man to try to do **"good works" apart from God's leadership and direction**.

Object Lesson: Show the students the candle (*or a cell phone*) and explain that this was man when God breathed life into him. (*mind, body, and spirit*) When they ate of the tree, their light was blown out—power source was gone. The candle does not have the ability to bring light and heat but has the parts to be (*ability*) lit again. (*needs a power source*)

Using a cell phone, make a call and then hang up. Take out the sim card and explain that the phone still works, but does not have the ability to communicate any longer with others. (*must have the sim card put back in to communicate*)

The Effects Of Sin

- If you **eat of the tree** of the knowledge of good and evil **you will die** (Genesis 2:16 &17) The wages/payment of sin is death (Romans 6:23)
- **What happened**? Their eyes were opened, to what? They knew good and evil, they were naked? God's presence departed (Genesis 3: 7)
- They lost their **knowing, seeing, power to do**
- The devil <u>deceived them into believing that God was withholding something good</u> from them, but in reality, God **did not want them to know good or evil.**
    - *(Example: Parents tell their children that they don't want them to do something and they do it anyway! Maybe you learn something you really didn't want to know) It leads to heart break.*
- **They hid themselves** (shame)—tried to cover it up! They heard God and were afraid, they knew they were naked and were afraid. They felt the presence of God depart; they didn't know what would happen next! They tried to sew fig leaves to cover themselves, but they knew they would not fool God. It wasn't because they had no clothes on, they felt the glory or covering of God leave, and they "felt naked"**.** (Genesis 3:8)
- In verse 10, they stood before him, waiting for physical death. (*whatever that meant*?)

- **Fear** (afraid of what would happen next) Adam knew death was his penalty. They were already feeling the first part of it with their eyes **being opened to good and evil and feeling separated from God** (spiritual death). (Genesis 3:10)
- Who told you that you were naked /uncovered?—guilty (Genesis 3:11)
- They blamed someone else, or did he actually blame God? (Genesis 3:11)
- They felt shame, guilt, fear, jealousy, violence, anger, hatred, care, responsibility, concern, burdened, worry, greed, lust, pain, etc.

They Hid From God and Blamed Each Other

Genesis 3:6-13 (NASB)—*When the woman saw that the tree was good for food, and that it was a delight to the eyes, and that the tree was desirable to make one wise, she took from its fruit and ate; and she gave also to her husband with her, and he ate. Then the eyes of both of them were opened, and they knew that they were naked; and they sewed fig leaves together and made themselves loin coverings. They heard the sound of the Lord God walking in the garden in the cool of the day, and the man and his wife hid themselves from the presence of the Lord God among the trees of the garden. Then the Lord God called to the man, and said to him, "Where are you?" He said, "I heard the sound of You in the garden, and I was afraid because I was naked; so I hid myself." And He said, "Who told you that you were naked? Have you eaten from the tree of which I commanded you not to eat?" The man said, "The woman whom You gave to be with me, she gave me from the tree, and I ate." Then the Lord God said to the woman, "What is this you have done?" And the woman said, "The serpent deceived me, and I ate."*

God Cursed The Serpent And Punished Adam And Eve

- The Punishment and the Curse (Genesis 3:14 –19)
- Punishment - God came and punished Adam and Eve and cursed the serpent and the earth.

Serpent

- Cursed it to its belly and to live in the ground
- Prophecies his future defeat by the woman's child (redeemer would come and defeat you)

- Enmity between the Serpent and the woman

Eve

- Pain with childbirth
- Prophecies that her seed will defeat the enemy (vs. 15)

Adam

- Work for your food
- Bodies would turn back to dust - Physical death (they were intended to live forever)
- God didn't want them to live forever with this "knowledge of good and evil" so they had to die. (*It would be like you knowing your dog was suffering, but wishing it could live forever. Kind of mean...)*

The Curse Brought...

- Sickness, fear, strife, jealousy, violence, death, anger, hatred, shame, worry, sadness, hopelessness, loss of security, trust and joy etc.
- The **animals**: caused the animals to go into survival mode/self-preservation! (*now they sting and bite and hunt one another to survive*)
- The **earth**—to produce thistles, thorns, weeds, destructive weather patterns (*earth quakes, tornadoes, hurricanes, tsunamis, volcanoes*)

God Kicks Adam & Eve Out of the Garden

Genesis 3:21-24 (NASB)—*The Lord God made garments of skin for Adam and his wife, and clothed them. Then the Lord God said, "Behold, the man has become like one of Us, knowing good and evil; and now, he might stretch out his hand, and take also from the tree of life, and eat, and live forever" therefore the Lord God sent him out from the garden of Eden, to cultivate the ground from which he was taken. So He drove the man out; and at the east of the garden of Eden He stationed the cherubim and the flaming sword which turned every direction to guard the way to the tree of life.*

- God never intended for man to live "knowing evil" forever (Genesis 3:22) So God stopped man from eating from **the tree of life** ever again. (physical death began)
- **Tree of Life**—was an antidote against disease and bodily decay, if they kept eating the fruit from the tree, they would have lived forever **knowing good and evil and God did not want them to live helplessly in a sinful state**.

What To Do?

- They are separated from God, and their bodies are slowly dying.
- They are "living being" so they will live forever somewhere?
- They are separated from God so they can't go to heaven.

ALL Of Mankind Are Born As Sinners

Romans 5:12 (NASB 1995)—*Therefore, just as through one man sin entered into the world, and death through sin, and so death spread to all men, because all sinned.*

- Thru **one act** of disobedience, all men are born sinners and have a sinful nature.

They Need A Savior!

John 3:16 (NASB 1995)—*"For God so loved the world, that He gave His only begotten Son, that whoever believes in Him shall not perish, but have eternal life."*

Each one of us is created like Adam & Eve; we are all born into sin. We are living souls just like them; we will live forever.

The question is: Where will it be? *Heaven or Hell?*

LESSON # 3: THE REMEDY FOR DEATH

Supplies: Knife, bowl, stuffed or live animal, (if you bring a live animal you may want to hide animal until you are ready to do your demonstration otherwise you will lose your group) fake fur or mink stole.

Give each student a piece of paper with a wrong done and ask them what punishment they think they deserve! (*lying, stealing, rape, cheating on a final exam, fighting, robbing a bank, carrying an illegal gun, bullying a special needs person, driving a car without a license, underage drinking, selling illegal drugs.)*

Discussion Question

Every wrong deed deserves a punishment, right?

Recap From Last Lesson

Last week, we talked about what happened to Adam and Eve when they disobeyed God and ate the fruit of the tree of the knowledge of good and evil. We saw how sin entered in and that they saw and felt (pleasures—good) and evil (RA). Through one act of sin, all of mankind is born into the world as sinners without God.

God Said...

Genesis 2:16-17 (NASB 1995)—*The Lord God commanded the man, saying, "From any tree of the garden you may eat freely; but from the tree of the knowledge of good and evil you shall not eat, for in the day that you eat from it you will surely die."*

The Serpent (The Devil) Said...

Genesis 3:4-5 (NASB 1995)—*The serpent said to the woman, "You surely will not die! For God knows that in the day you eat from it your* ***eyes*** *will be* ***opened****, and you will be like God,* ***knowing*** *good and evil."*

Eve (The Woman) Said...

Genesis 3:6 (NASB 1995)—*When the woman saw that the tree was good for food, and that it was a delight to the eyes, and that the tree was desirable to make one wise, she took from its fruit and ate; and she gave also to her husband with her, and he ate. 7 Then the eyes of both of them were opened, and they knew that they were naked; and they sewed fig leaves together and made themselves loin coverings. 8 They heard the sound of the Lord God walking in the garden in the cool of the day, and the man and his wife hid themselves from the presence of the Lord God among the trees of the garden.*

Did They Die? Yes And No

- Spiritually they (died) were separated from God.
- Physically, not right away, but the death process began.

God Cursed The Serpent And Punished Adam And Eve!

- **Genesis 3:14–19**
- God **punished Adam and Eve** and **cursed the serpent** and **the earth**.

Serpent

- Cursed it to its belly and to live in the ground
- Prophecies his future defeat by the woman's seed (a redeemer would come and defeat you)
- Enmity between the Serpent and the woman

Eve

- Pain with childbirth
- Prophecy—that her child will defeat the enemy (vs. 15)

Adam

- Work for your food
- Bodies would turn back to dust—**Physical death** (they were intended to live forever). God didn't want them to live forever with this **"knowledge of good and evil"** so they had to die. (*It would be like you knowing your dog was suffering but wishing it could live forever—kind of mean.*)

Today's Lesson: The First Blood Sacrifice

What was the punishment for eating from the tree of the knowledge of good & evil?

> **Genesis 3:21-24** (NASB)—*And the LORD God made garments of skin for Adam and his wife, and clothed them. Then the LORD God said, "Behold, the man has become like one of Us, knowing good and evil; and now, he might reach out with his hand, and take fruit also from the tree of life, and eat, and live forever"—therefore the LORD God sent him out of the Garden of Eden, to cultivate the ground from which he was taken. So He drove the man out; and at the east of the Garden of Eden He stationed the cherubim and the flaming sword which turned every direction to guard the way to the tree of life.*

Why Did God Make Garments Of Skin And Clothe Them?

- V.21—after the punishment, He clothed them?
- Their payment for sin was death! (Gen 2:17- they would die!)
- God had **mercy** on them (undeserved) because He loved them
- What was the punishment?
- He took the coats and put the warm, bloody coats upon them.
- Where did he get them? Their companions!

Introduction

Ask each student to share with the class what kind of pets they have. (If students don't have an animal, talk about the things they love—a best friend, sibling, parent, etc.)

Arrange ahead of time to bring a pet *(ask a student if you don't have one or if you are unable to bring it to class*) into your classroom and demonstrate what God would have done to the animal.

Supplies: knife, bowl, animal (or stuffed)

Pretend to take the pet, slice its neck, skin it and place the hot skins on the back of the owner! (bring a mink or rabbit fur coat and lay it on the back of a student)

Death! Somebody Needed To Die!

Can you imagine that each time you made a decision to sin, one of your friends would be killed to cover it?

God provided the **first** and **last** sacrifice (first animal and His only son Jesus)

Why Did God Do That?

- Because **death was their penalty** and the only way to pay it is with death. (a life for death)
- He didn't want them to die, He wanted them to live and re-populate the earth.

Life Is In The Blood

- He **exchanged** life with death or death with life (***Law of first mention***: *this is the first time this is mentioned in the Bible and you will see a pattern throughout the Word*).
- **Hebrews 9:22** says, all things are cleansed with blood, without the shedding of blood there is no forgiveness of sin. (*example – if we were to drain all of our blood from our body we would die, it's because life is in the blood*)
- Adam and Eve had never seen death before (*this was the first murder*)
- They knew that their innocent animals had been put to death for them (Genesis 3:21)

The Blood Of Bulls And Goats Covered Sin

Hebrews 10:4 (NASB)—"For it is impossible for the blood of bulls and goats to take away sins". *(they only cover)*

- After the original sacrifice, God instructed them, when they sinned, it would require the life of an **innocent** lamb to forgive the sin of the **guilty**.
- The blood would **cover the sin** and **prevent judgment or punishment for that sin**.

A Sacrifice That Takes Away Our Sin

- God promised to send a savior to destroy the work of the devil and ***take away*** the sins of mankind. (Genesis 3:15)

Romans 3:23 (NASB)—*For all have sinned and come short of the glory of God.*

- When Jesus came, he took away our sins, not just covered them.

John 1:29 (NASB)—"The next day he saw *Jesus coming to him, and said, "Behold, the Lamb of God who takes away the sins of the world!")*

II Cor. 5:21 (NASB)—*He made Him who knew no sin to be sin on our behalf, that we might become the righteousness of God in Him.* (*Innocent for the guilty – exchange*)

- He died for us; he took our punishment for us!

I John 1:9 (KJV)—*If we confess our sins, he is faithful and just to forgive us our sins, and to cleanse us from all unrighteousness.*

- We must apply the blood; Jesus shed his blood for everyone…but not everyone accepts it!

The Remedy For Sin

John 3:16 (ESV)—*For God so loved the world, that he gave his only Son, that whoever believes in him should not perish but have eternal life.*

LESSON # 4: THE ORIGIN OF SIN

Introduction

Hand out The Devil Survey. Each person will fill it out and discuss their answers (*attached to the bottom of this lesson).*

Review

Over the last several weeks, we have been talking about Adam and Eve and them being tempted by the serpent (Devil) to eat of the forbidden fruit.

Where Did The Devil Come From?

You answered the questions on the Devil Survey, and all had a lot of right answers but a lot of wrong ones too.

Let's Get To The Truth—Lucifer In Heaven

> **Ezekiel 28:12b-18** (NASB)—*"Son of man, take up a lament concerning the king of Tyre and say to him: 'This is what the Sovereign Lord says:*
>
> *" 'You were the seal of perfection, full of wisdom and perfect in beauty. You were in Eden, the garden of God; every precious stone adorned you: carnelian, chrysolite and emerald, topaz, onyx and jasper, lapis lazuli, turquoise and beryl. Your settings and mountings were made of gold; on the day you were created they were prepared. You were anointed as a guardian cherub, for so I ordained you. You were on the holy mount of God; you walked among the fiery stones. You were blameless in your ways from the day you were created till wickedness was found in you. Through your widespread trade you were filled with violence, and you sinned. So I drove you in disgrace from the mount of God, and I expelled you, guardian cherub, from*

among the fiery stones. Your heart became proud on account of your beauty, and you corrupted your wisdom because of your splendor. So I threw you to the earth; I made a spectacle of you before kings. By your many sins and dishonest trade you have desecrated your sanctuaries. So I made a fire come out from you, and it consumed you, and I reduced you to ashes on the ground in the sight of all who were watching.

Lucifer (His Name Before He Sinned) Was Created By God

- **Full of wisdom** and **perfect in beauty** (knowledge & pride)
- Made of precious **gems and gold** ($)
- Workmanship was **made into settings of flutes & tambourines** (He was created to lead worship—made of instruments—music)
- *Muse* means: a guiding spirit—A source of inspiration
- He was the **angel that "covers" in the holy place of God** (#1 angel) **guarded the mercy seat**
- He was a Keeper of the Law and tries to take us back to works.
- Blameless until unrighteousness was found in you.
- Kicked out of the mountain of God **because your heart was lifted up** because of your beauty; **you corrupted your wisdom by reason of your splendor**.

Lucifer was called the "archangel that covered". This is a picture of the two angels positioned on the ark in heaven. Lucifer is the accuser of the brethren, and theoretically, his job was to make sure the law was kept. Those who broke the law were prosecuted and judged.

Why Lucifer Was Kicked Out Of Heaven

Isaiah 14:11-14 (NASB)—*"'Now you are as weak as we are! Your might and power were buried with you. The sound of the harp in your palace has ceased. Now maggots are your sheet, and worms your blanket.'*

"How you are fallen from heaven, O shining star, son of the morning! You have been thrown down to the earth, you who destroyed the nations of the world. For you said to yourself, 'I will ascend to heaven and set my throne above God's stars. I will preside on the mountain of the gods far away in the north. I will climb to the highest heavens and be like the Most High.'

Isaiah 14:12 (KJV)—*How art thou fallen from heaven, O Lucifer, son of the morning! how art thou cut down to the ground, which didst weaken the nations!* (Where we get the name Lucifer)

Isaiah 14:13-15 (NASB)—*"But you said in your heart, 'I will ascend to heaven; I will raise my throne above the stars of God, And I will sit on the mount of assembly In the recesses of the north.*

'I will ascend above the heights of the clouds; I will make myself like the Most High.'

"Nevertheless you will be brought down to Sheol, To the recesses of the pit.

Isaiah 14:13-14 (ASV)—*And thou saidst in thy heart,* ***I will*** *ascend into heaven,* ***I will*** *exalt my throne above the stars of God; and* ***I will*** *sit upon the mount of congregation, in the uttermost parts of the north; I will ascend above the heights of the clouds; I will make myself like the Most High.*

What Lucifer Did

- He was in rebellion
- And was full of Pride—**I will, I will, I will** (*ascend, exalt, sit*)

Lucifer's Heavenly Position

Ezekiel 28:12-18 (KJV)—*Son of man, take up a lamentation upon the king of Tyrus, and say unto him, Thus saith the Lord GOD; Thou sealest up the sum, full of wisdom, and perfect in beauty.*

Thou hast been in Eden the garden of God; every precious stone was thy covering, the sardius, topaz, and the diamond, the beryl, the onyx, and the jasper, the sapphire, the emerald, and the carbuncle, and gold: the workmanship of thy tabrets and of thy pipes was prepared in thee in the day that thou wast created.

Thou art the anointed cherub that covereth; and I have set thee so: thou wast upon the holy mountain of God; thou hast walked up and down in the midst of the stones of fire.

Thou wast perfect in thy ways from the day that thou wast created, till iniquity was found in thee.

By the multitude of thy merchandise they have filled the midst of thee with violence, and thou hast sinned: therefore I will cast thee as profane out of the mountain of God: and I will destroy thee, O covering cherub, from the midst of the stones of fire.

Thine heart was lifted up because of thy beauty, thou hast corrupted thy wisdom by reason of thy brightness: I will cast thee to the ground, I will lay thee before kings, that they may behold thee.

Thou hast defiled thy sanctuaries by the multitude of thine iniquities, by the iniquity of thy traffick; therefore will I bring forth a fire from the midst of thee, it shall devour thee, and I will bring thee to ashes upon the earth in the sight of all them that behold thee.

Read aloud and examine Ezekiel 28:12b-18...

- Vs. 14—anointed cherub (high priest position) privilege to stand in the presence of God. He went on behalf of the people—keeper of the law. **Revelation 12:10**—Accuser
- Vs. 13b—created with instrument in his being —he was created **to worship God.** ("tabrets" is timbrel/tambourine in Hebrew and "pipes" is groove, socket, hole, cavity, settings. Likely a flute like instrument.
- Vs. 17—he was full of wisdom

What Happened? He Had It All!

- V.15—Guilt was found in him.
- Vs. 16—He was greedy and chose to sin.
- Vs. 17—Prideful
- Vs. 17—He corrupted his wisdom because he thought he was so wonderful, he now uses his wisdom in evil—deceiving, scheming, lying, perverting the truth.

- Lucifer had it all and lost it because ***he wanted to be worshipped*** instead of a worshipper (he didn't want to obey authority / he wanted to be the authority)
  - position
  - beauty
  - honor as the anointed cherub that covers
  - favor of God

Lucifer And 1/3 Of The Angels Are Cast Out Of Heaven

Rev. 12:7-9 (NASB)—*And there was war in heaven, Michael and his angels waging war with the dragon.* ***The dragon and his angels*** *waged war, and they did not prevail, and there was no longer a place found for them in heaven. And the* ***great dragon*** *was thrown down, the serpent of old who is called the devil and Satan, who deceives the whole world; he was thrown down to the earth, and his angels were thrown down with him.*

- Michael and his angels (Gods) waged war with Lucifer and his angels (Lucifer's). Michael kicked Lucifer and his angels out of heaven and cast them to earth.

Revelation 12:7-10

- Lucifer **loses his name** and is now referred to as the serpent of old, Satan or devil.

Satan Becomes The Ruler Of This Earth

John 12:30-32 (NASB)—*Jesus responded and said, "This voice has not come for My sake, but for yours. Now judgment is upon this world; now the ruler of this world will be cast out. And I, if I am lifted up from the earth, will draw all people to Myself."*

- Satan now uses his wisdom for evil—he is crafty, sneaky and deceitful (Ezekiel 28:17)
- Satan still wants to be like God. He is always looking for ways to get people to worship him instead of God.

The devil hasn't changed, and we should not be ignorant of his schemes

Many Worship Satan Unaware Through Music

Music has a powerful influence in our society today. Many people worship the Devil and obey him thru it without even knowing it; most people would not knowingly or willingly worship the Devil or obey him.

- **Isaiah 14:11**—your pomp and the **music** of your harps have been brought down to Sheol.
- **Lucifer** was created with **musical instruments in his being**, to lead the angels in worship.
- **Ephesians 2:2**—Calls Satan (Lucifer) the **prince of the power of the air**. He uses the airwaves, music, and entertainment industry to seduce, deceive and turn the hearts of man to worship him (entertainer) instead of God.

Music: Meaning of Music is the root word muse: A guiding spirit., A source of inspiration

Inspiration: Meaning of Inspiration is to produce or arouse (a feeling, thought, etc.) to influence or impel, to fill or affect with a specified feeling; thought to guide or control by divine influence; to prompt or instigate (utterances, acts, etc.) by influence, without avowal of responsibility.

Satan Uses His Spirit To Guide And Inspire Singers And Songwriters To Create Music That We Listen To Today!

2 Corinthians 4:4 (NASB)—*in whose case the god of this world has blinded the minds of the unbelieving so that they will not see the light of the gospel of the glory of Christ, who is the image of God.*

- ALL Music has a message.
- Styles of music (Rap, R&B, County, hard Rock & Roll, Pop, etc.) it is not the style or genera of music that is in question. The question to ask when listening to music is the source of inspiration. Is it God or the Devil?
- The music we listen to over & over shares its message with us.
- You agree with the message, inspiring you to "do" the message.
- What is he inspiring you to sing? To do?
- Many of you listen to music all day and night; you are hearing the message of that music and agreeing with it. Watch the message you are hearing!

- Satan uses **the music and entertainment industry as one of his tools to distract and influence humanity** away from the worship of God by presenting "idols" to be worshipped. If he can get people to worship others, they inadvertently worship him.

Assignment

Pick out a popular **secular song of the day** and a **worship song** and look at the words (*read the words to each*)

- Each has a **message**, and each **inspires** people to act.
- Dissect both songs
    - **Secular song:** inspires **rebellion against God and His Word** and inadvertently worshiping the **Devil**.
    - **Christian song:** inspires obedience and **worship toward God**.

Closure

Sometimes we make excuses about "our" music, "It's only country, it's not so bad," or, "It's only a love song." Is it inspiring you to reminisce about an old love lost and making you feel lonely or depressed? …inspiring you to cheat, lust, drown your sorrows, cry, etc.? Remember, all music has a message and inspires action.

THE DEVIL SURVEY

Questions:

1. What was the Devil's original name?
2. Do God and the Devil have equal powers?
3. Who does the Devil rule?
4. The Devil is known as the father of what?
5. Is the Devil Jesus' brother?
6. Describe what you think the Devil looks like.
7. Do you think the Devil is real or fiction or a myth?
8. Do you think the Devil has power?
9. What kind of power does he have?
10. Can the Devil perform miracles?
11. Is the Devil a human, angel, or a god?
12. Is the Devil in hell now?
13. Do you know what will happen to the Devil in the future? If so, describe it…

Answer Key:

1. What was the Devil's original name?

   Lucifer was the original Hebrew name for "son of the dawn" in **Isaiah 14:12,** and translated into the 21st Century King James Version of the Bible.

2. Do God and the Devil have equal power?

   No, Lucifer was created by God as an angel to minister to God **(Ezekiel 28:13)** The angels were created a little lower than man **(Psm 8:3**)

3. Who does the Devil rule?

   Fallen angels or demons **(Matt. 9:34; Mark 3:22)** and the ruler of this world **(John 12:31;14:30; 16:11),** the sons of disobedience **(Eph. 2:2)**

4. The Devil is known as the father of lies - **(John 8:44)**

5. Is the Devil Jesus' brother?

   No, Jesus is God, and they created the angels **(John 1:1)**

6. Describe what you think the Devil looks like…

   He was created beautiful **(Ez. 28:12-13),** after the his fall he comes in many forms (**Genesis 3:1– shining one),** the dragon or serpent of old **(Revelation 12:9**); and the beast in **(Revelation 13:1-18)**

7. Do you think the Devil is real or fiction or a myth?

   If you are a Christian then you believe the Bible when it says he exists. **In II Tim. 3:4**, it says that all scripture is **inspired or breathed by God** and profitable for teaching, for reproof, for correction, for training in righteousness.

8. Do you think the Devil has power?

   Yes, he does….examples: **Revelation 13:2** "And the dragon gave the beast his power".

9. What kind of powers does he have?

1) He is known as the prince of the power of the air, primary power is to influence mindsets or how people think. **Eph. 2:2** (airwaves - TV, radio, satelites) Religions – antichrist.

2) Sickness, disease and infirmities **(Luke 13:11, Matt:1)**

10. Can the Devil perform miracles?

    Revelations 13:11-15 "He preformed great signs".

11. Is the Devil a human, angel, or a god?

    He was created as the anointed cherub (angel) that covers. **Ezekiel 28:14**

12. Is the Devil in hell now?

    No, he roams the earth looking for whom he can devour. **I Peter 5:8**

13. Do you know what will happen to the Devil in the future? If so, describe it.

    In Revelation 20:1-3; Revelation 20:7-10, the devil is bound for a thousand years and thrown into the abyss with a seal over it. After a thousand years, he is released for a short time to deceive the nations of the four corners of the earth, and then he is thrown into the lake of fire to be tormented day and night.

LESSON # 5: CAIN AND ABEL—THE LINEAGE OF CHRIST

Cain And Abel

Genesis 4:1-5 (NASB)—*Now the man had relations with his wife Eve, and she conceived and gave birth to Cain, and she said, "I have obtained a male child with the help of the Lord." And again, she gave birth to his brother Abel. Now Abel was a keeper of flocks, but Cain was a cultivator of the ground. So it came about in the course of time that Cain brought an offering to the Lord from the fruit of the ground.*

Abel, on his part also brought an offering, from the firstborn of his flock and from their fat portions. And the Lord had regard for Abel and his offering; but for Cain and his offering He had no regard. So Cain became very angry and his face was gloomy.

- Abel was a shepherd
- Cain was a farmer
- It was harvest time, a time to give their first fruits to the Lord
- Cain brought his offering from the garden
- Abel gave of the firstborn of his flock

The Lord had "regard" (to look at) for Abel's offering.

But for Cain's offering, he had "no regard" (not able to look at).

Discussion Questions

1. Do you think God's reaction was fair?

2. Would you be mad if you were Cain? *(He worked so hard and gave his best gift to God and God wouldn't even look at it!)*
3. Why do you think God rejected Cain's offering?
4. What was missing from Cain's offering? (look at Vs. 4 The Firstlings of his flock & the Fat portion)
5. Why was it important that God accept the offering? Let's Find out!

The First Blood Covenant–When Adam & Eve (Their Parents) Sinned

Genesis 3:21 (NASB)—*And the Lord God made garments of skin for Adam and his wife, and clothed them.*

The penalty for sin is death; a life had to be taken so that they could live.

- God provided the first blood sacrifice to cover their sins.
- Afterward, each time sin was committed, man had to kill an animal and sprinkle its blood on the altar and repent of their sins to be right with God again.
- Adam & Eve taught their children the sacrificial system

Eventually, God set up a Priesthood to do all of the sacrificing (Below are their instructions)

Leviticus 3:16-17 (NASB)—*"'The priest shall offer them up in smoke on the altar as food, an offering by fire as a soothing aroma; all fat is the Lord's. It is a permanent statute throughout your generations in all your dwelling places: you shall not eat any fat or any blood.'"*

Sacrifice Under The Law

- Brought their animal to the priest
- They placed their hands on the animal's head and transferred their guilt (*wages of sin is death—exchange*)
- They cut the jugular vein
- Priest drained the blood and sprinkled it on the altar
- Priest carved the animal and remove the fat, entrails, liver and kidney and burned them on the altar.

Why Cain's Offering Was Rejected

Hebrews 9: 22 (NASB 1995)—*And according to the Law, one may almost say, all things are cleansed with blood, and without shedding of blood there is no forgiveness.*

Leviticus 3:16 (NASB 1995)—*The priest shall offer them up in smoke on the altar as food, an offering by fire for a soothing aroma; all fat is the LORD'S.* (first portion—sweet savor unto the Lord) Robbed God of His portion. It belonged to Him.

- The sacrificial process restored man back to God when they sinned.
- The blood is required to come into his presence, and the fat belongs to the LORD!

Can you see now why God could not look at the sacrifice?

Cain knew what sacrifice he should have brought to the Lord. To receive forgiveness of sin, blood was required, and that Fat portion was God's. It should have been no surprise to him when God could not look at his sacrifice and accept it. He stood before the altar as a sinner and a robber.

The Bible refers to the **"way of Cain"** as the **"way of self-will and unbelief"** (Jude 11).

Cain Is Banished

Genesis 4:5-15 (NASB)—*...but for Cain and for his offering He had no regard. So Cain became very angry and his countenance fell. Then the Lord said to Cain, "Why are you angry? And why has your countenance fallen? **If you do well**, will not your countenance be lifted up? And if you do not do well, sin is crouching at the door; and its desire is for you, but you must master it." Cain told Abel his brother. And it came about when they were in the field, that Cain rose up **against Abel his brother and killed him**.*

*Then the Lord said to Cain, "Where is Abel your brother?" And he said, "I do not know. Am I my brother's keeper?" He said, "What have you done? The voice of your brother's **blood is crying to Me from the ground.*** (life is in the blood) *Now **you are cursed from the ground**, which has opened its mouth to receive your brother's blood from your hand. When you cultivate the ground, it will no longer* *yield its strength to you; you will be a* ***vagrant and a wanderer*** *on the earth." Cain said to the Lord, "My punishment is too great to bear! Behold, You have driven me this day from the face of the ground; and from* ***Your face I will be hidden****, and I will be a vagrant and a wanderer on the earth, and whoever finds me will kill me." So the Lord said to him, "Therefore whoever kills Cain, vengeance will be taken on him sevenfold." And the Lord appointed a sign for Cain, so that no one finding him would slay him.*

The Prophecy From God To Eve And The Serpent?

Genesis 3:15 (NASB 1995*)—"And I will put enmity Between you and the woman, And between your seed and her seed; He shall bruise you on the head, And you shall bruise him on the heel."*

- **Abel is dead** (Genesis 4:8)
- **Cain is banished from God?**
    - **Genesis 4:16** (NASB 1995)—*Then Cain went out from the presence of the Lord, and settled in the land of Nod,* ***east of Eden.***
    - Eastern religions—interesting how many still don't shed blood, they are mostly vegetarians.
- **Seth**—the new offspring

Genesis 4:25-26 (NASB 1995)—*Adam had relations with his wife again; and she gave birth to a son, and named him Seth, for, she said, "God has appointed me another child in place of Abel, because Cain killed him." To Seth also a son was born; and he named him Enosh. Then people began to call upon the name of the LORD.*

Lineage Of Adam To Noah

Refer to the chart: **Genealogy of Adam**. Focus on Cain and note that his descendants were killed in the flood. (*except for Noah's daughter in laws*)

Let's See all of the events in the Bible where "**his seed**" tries to destroy "**her seed**." Then we will see how God protects the seed in the lineage of Eve. *(All of the major stories in the Bible)*

Throughout the entire Bible, God is a Promise Keeper and a Way Maker!

Adam

Genesis 3:15 (NASB 1995)—*"And I will put enmity between you and the woman, and between your seed and her seed; he shall bruise you on the head, and you shall bruise him on the heel."*

Cain Kills Abel

Genesis 4:8 (NASB 1995)—*Cain told Abel his brother. And it came about when they were in the field, that Cain rose up against Abel his brother and killed him.*

- Righteous seed born—***Seth***
- Adamic Covenant

Noah (See The Chart: Bible Nations Descended From Noah's Sons)

- The Devil perverted mankind (Genesis 6)
- God saves the only righteous
- Noah's Covenant (Genesis 9)
- ***Shem,*** Ham & Japheth ***(see chart below)***

Abraham's Lineage

See the chart: **Jacob's Extended Family Tree**

Abraham

- Listens to the voice of his wife (Sarah—Lot's sister) and has a child named Ishmael. (Genesis 15)
- God gives him the promised son Isaac. Divided nations by hooking up with Heathen/Egyptian woman. (Genesis 16)
- Abrahamic Covenant (Genesis 17)

Isaac & Rebecca Have Twin Sons–Jacob & Esau

- Esau hooked up with Heathen women—***Edomites***
- Covenant with Jacob—changed his name to Israel (Genesis 35)
- Jacob is deceived into marrying the sister (Leah) of the woman he loves and eventually the one he loves (Rachel)—***12 sons become the 12 tribes of Israel***

Judah (Promised Savior Thru Judah's Seed) & Tamar (Genesis 38)

- Had to have a seed on the earth to fulfill the Prophecy
- Genesis 49:10

Israel Settles In Egypt

- Pharaoh tries to kill all of the male babies (kill the seed)
- Moses is raised up ***(tribe of Levi)***
- Mosaic Covenant

King Saul

- Men rejected God and demanded a King—tribe of Benjamin
- King David—the tribe of Judah—Jesus
- Promised king (Isaiah 11:10)
- Acts 13:22-23
- Davidic Covenant (II Samuel 7:8)

King David's Lineage

See the chart: **Genealogy of the Kings of Judah & Israel**

Solomon

- Kingdom divided by hooking up with Heathen women (I Kings 11:9-13)
- Rehoboam became the King of Judah ***(Jacob/Israel—Judah's seed)***
- Jeroboam (He was an *Edomite/Esau* & married an Egyptian King's daughter) became the king of Israel.

Esther

- Slaughter of the Jews
- Haman the Agagite plotted to kill all of the Jews—Amalekite (I Samuel 15)
- God raised up Esther and Mordecai to thwart the plot—***tribe of Benjamin; same tribe of King Saul***

Jesus' Lineage

See the chart: **Genealogy of Jesus**

Jesus

- All male babies were to be killed
- Jesus died on the cross
- Devil thought he had finally killed him
- Fulfillment of all the Covenants

Church

- Promises to return for us (Revelations 5:5)

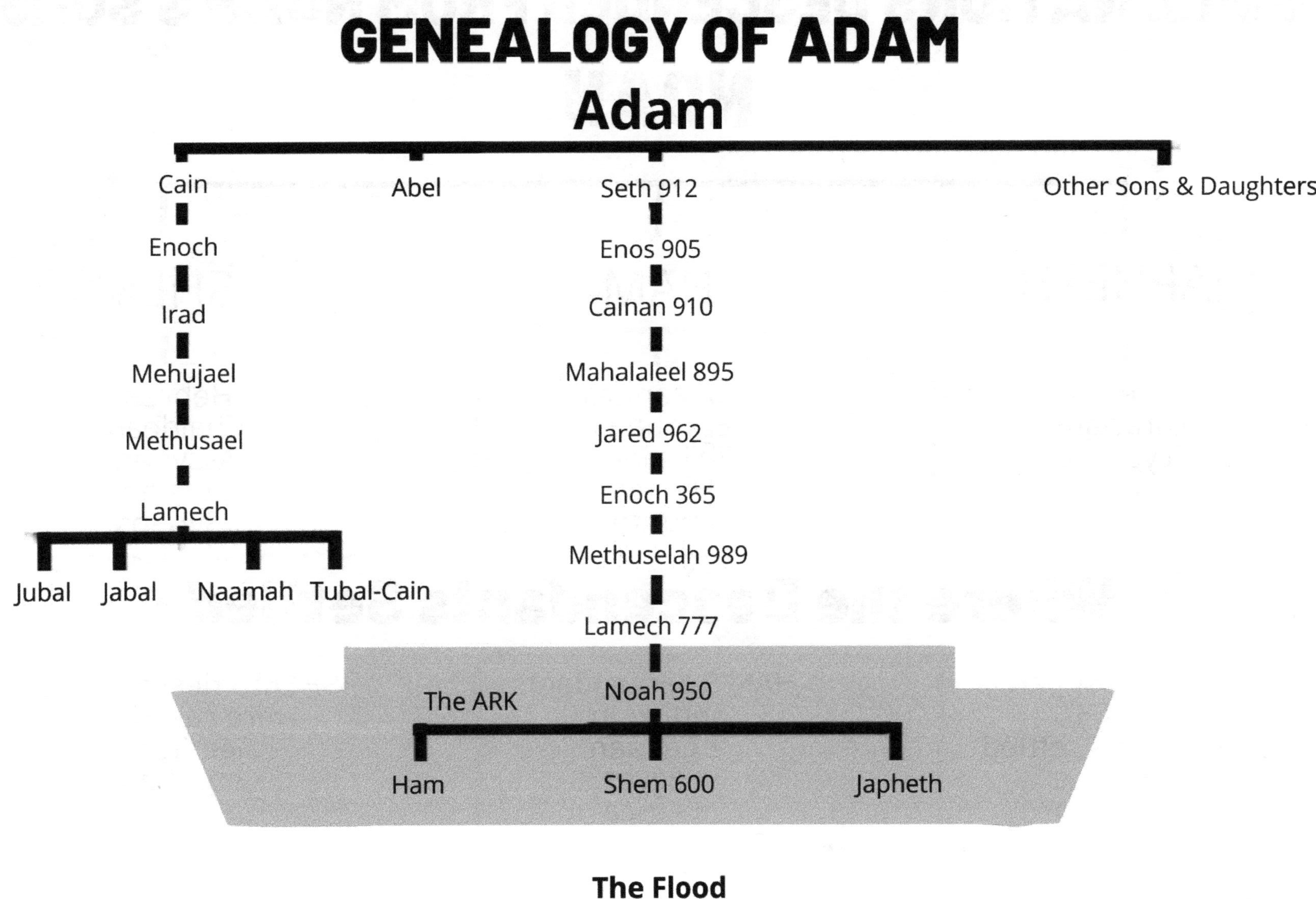
GENEALOGY OF ADAM
Adam
Cain
Abel
Seth 912
Other Sons & Daughters
Enoch
Irad
Mehujael
Methusael
Lamech
Jubal
Jabal
Naamah
Tubal-Cain
Enos 905
Cainan 910
Mahalaleel 895
Jared 962
Enoch 365
Methuselah 989
Lamech 777
Noah 950
The ARK
Ham
Shem 600
Japheth
The Flood

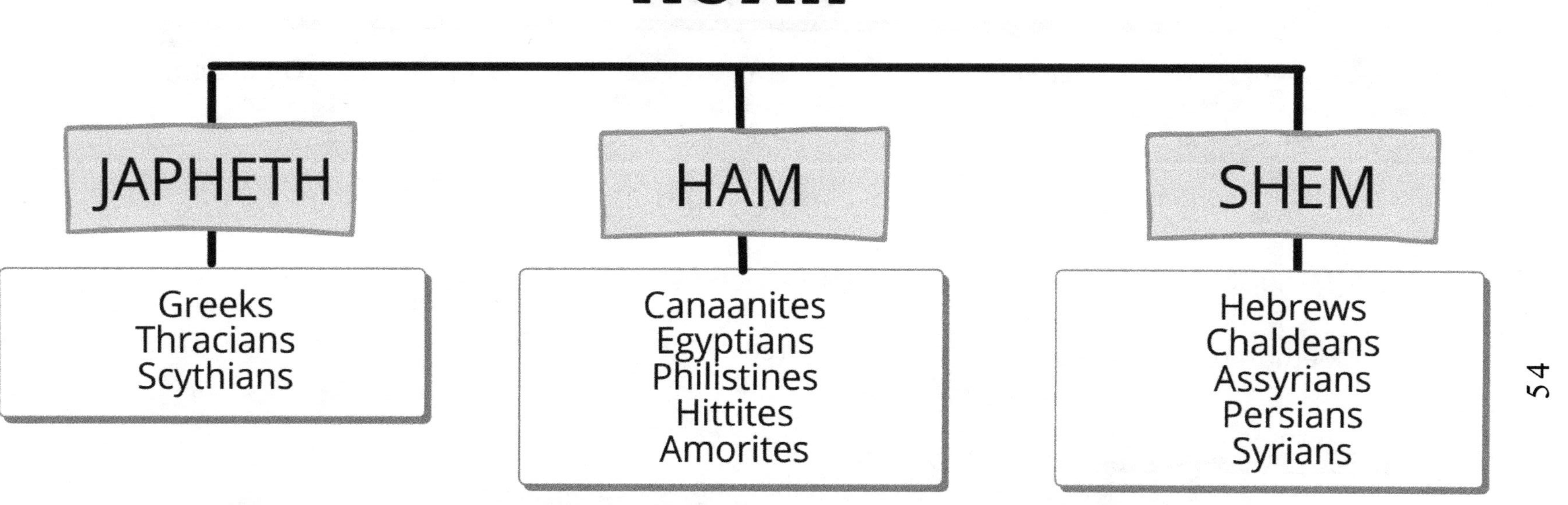
BIBLE NATIONS DESCENDED FROM NOAH'S SONS
NOAH
JAPHETH
HAM
SHEM
Greeks
Thracians
Scythians
Canaanites
Egyptians
Philistines
Hittites
Amorites
Hebrews
Chaldeans
Assyrians
Persians
Syrians
Where the Descendants Settled
For the most part, JAPHETH'S descendants settled in • Europe • Asia Minor
HAM'S descendants settled in • Canaan • Egypt • Africa
SHEM'S descendants were called the Semites: • Abraham • Isaac • Jacob • David • Jesus

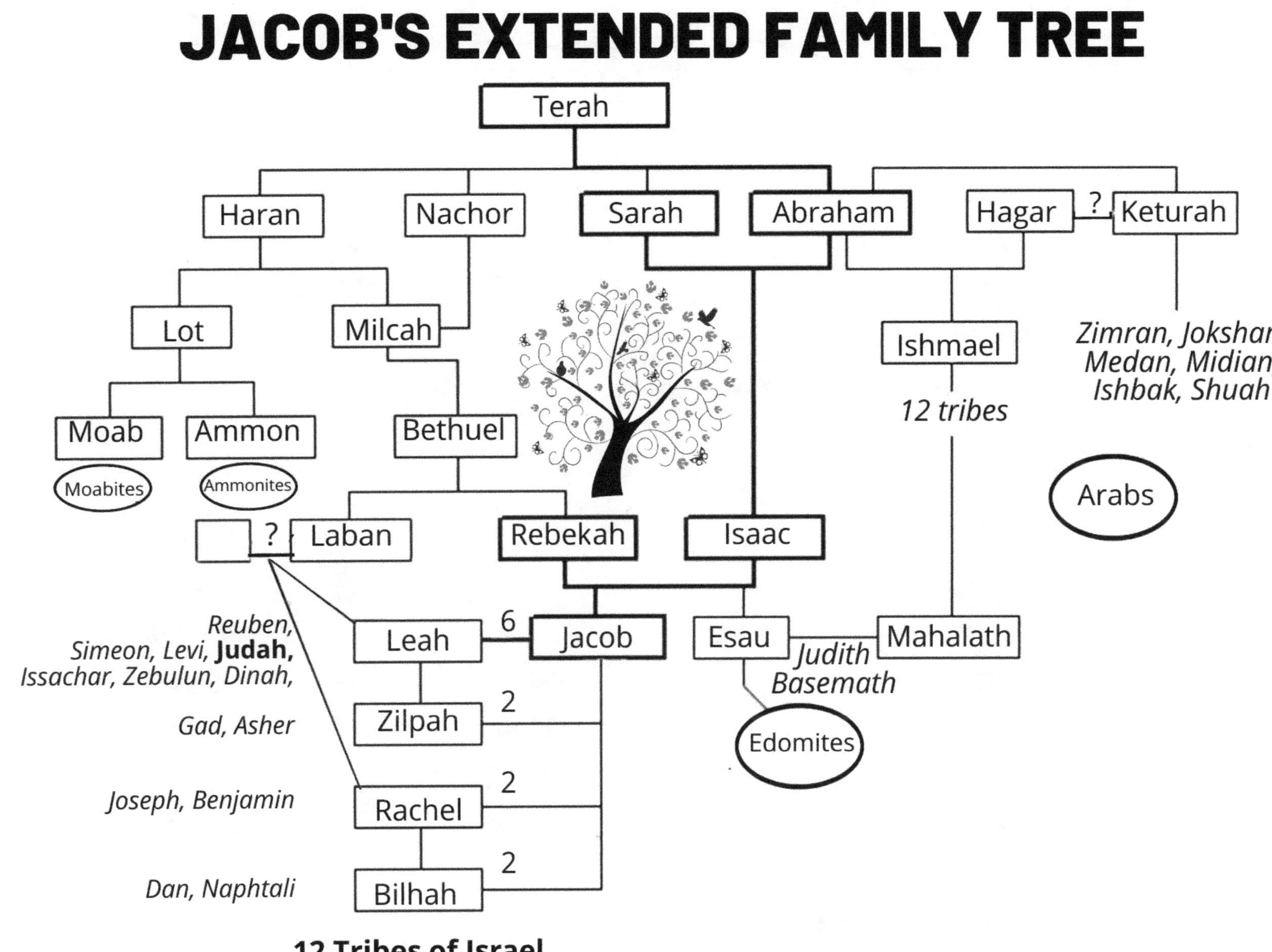
JACOB'S EXTENDED FAMILY TREE
Terah
Haran
Nachor
Sarah
Abraham
Hagar
?
Keturah
Lot
Milcah
Ishmael
Zimran, Jokshan, Medan, Midian, Ishbak, Shuah
12 tribes
Moab
Ammon
Bethuel
Moabites
Ammonites
Arabs
?
Laban
Rebekah
Isaac
Reuben, Simeon, Levi, Judah, Issachar, Zebulun, Dinah,
Leah
6
Jacob
Esau
Mahalath
Judith
Basemath
Gad, Asher
Zilpah
2
Edomites
Joseph, Benjamin
Rachel
2
Dan, Naphtali
Bilhah
2
12 Tribes of Israel

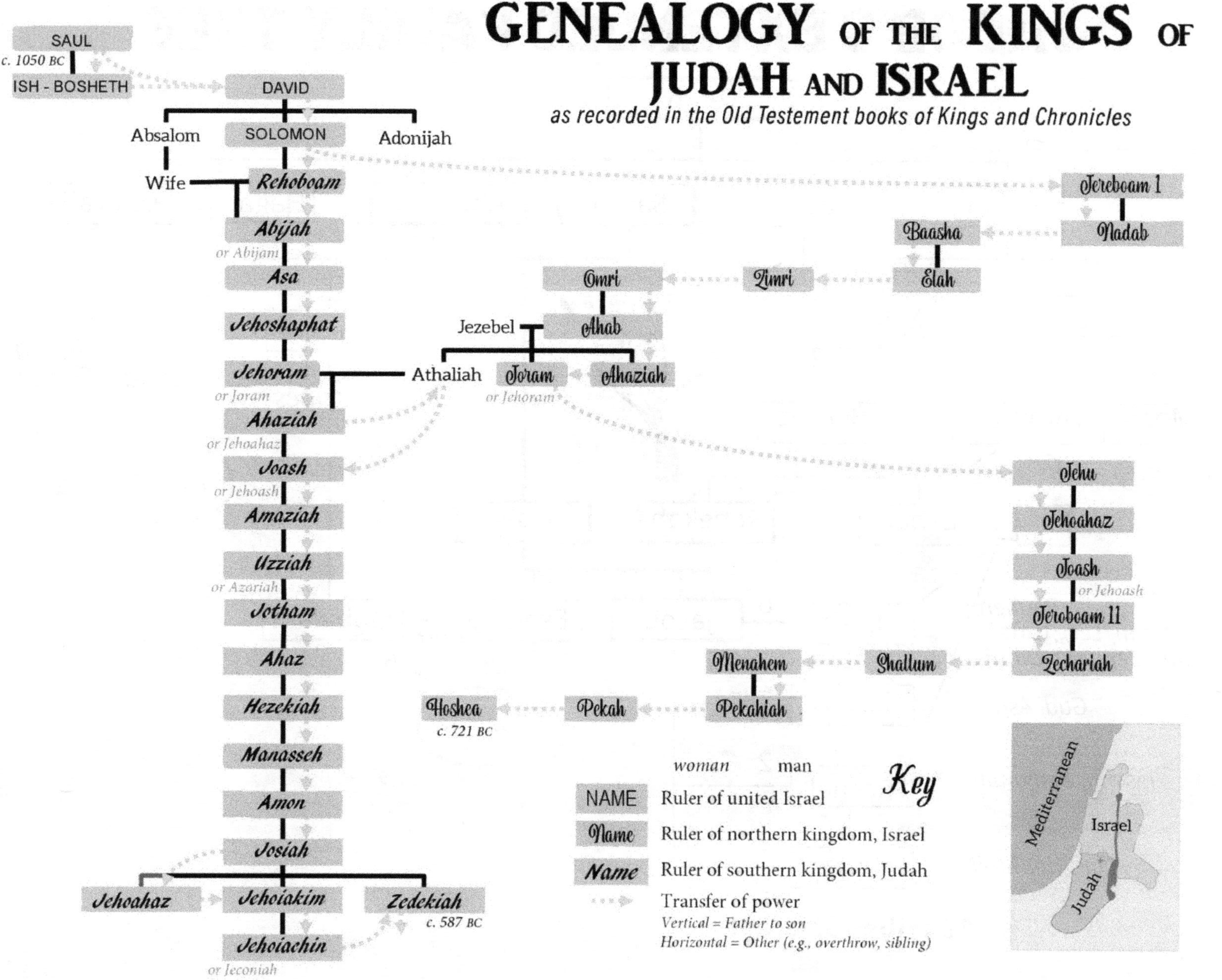

GENEALOGY OF THE KINGS OF JUDAH AND ISRAEL
as recorded in the Old Testement books of Kings and Chronicles
SAUL
c. 1050 BC
ISH - BOSHETH
DAVID
Absalom
SOLOMON
Adonijah
Wife
Rehoboam
Abijah
or Abijam
Asa
Jehoshaphat
Jehoram
or Joram
Ahaziah
or Jehoahaz
Joash
or Jehoash
Amaziah
Uzziah
or Azariah
Jotham
Ahaz
Hezekiah
Manasseh
Amon
Josiah
Jehoahaz
Jehoiakim
Zedekiah
c. 587 BC
Jehoiachin
or Jeconiah
Jereboam 1
Nadab
Baasha
Elah
Zimri
Omri
Ahab
Jezebel
Athaliah
Joram
or Jehoram
Ahaziah
Jehu
Jehoahaz
Joash
or Jehoash
Jeroboam II
Zechariah
Shallum
Menahem
Pekahiah
Pekah
Hoshea
c. 721 BC
woman
man
Key
NAME
Ruler of united Israel
Name
Ruler of northern kingdom, Israel
Name
Ruler of southern kingdom, Judah
Transfer of power
Vertical = Father to son
Horizontal = Other (e.g., overthrow, sibling)
Mediterranean
Israel
Judah

GENEALOGY OF JESUS
From Adam to Christ

ADAM
(4004 BC - 3074 BC)

Seth
Enosh
Kenan
Mahalalel
Jared
Enoch
Methuselah
Lamech

NOAH
(2948 BC - 1998 BC)

Shem
Arphaxad
Salah
Eber
Peleg
Reu
Serug
Nahor
Terah

ABRAHAM
(1996 BC-1821 BC)

Isaac
Jacob
Judah
Perez
Hezron
Ram
Amminadab
Nahshon
Salmon
Boaz
Obed
Jesse

KING DAVID
(1085 BC - 1015BC)

LINE OF JOSEPH (LUKE 3:23-38)

Nathan (he gave)
Mattatha
Menna
Melea
Eliakim
Jonam
Joseph
Judah
Simeon

Levi
Matthat
Jorim
Eliezer
Joshua
Er
Elmadam
Cosam
Addi

Melchi
Neri
Shealtiel
Zerubbabel
Rhesa
Joanan
Joda
Josech
Semein

Mattathias
Maath
Naggai
Hesli
Nahum
Amos
Mattathias
Joseph
Jannai

Melchi
Levi
Matthat
Eli
Mary

JESUS CHRIST
(5 BC - 33AD)

LINE OF MARY (MATT. 1)

Solomon (peace)
Rehoboam
Abijah
Asa
Jehoshaphat
Joram

Ahaziah
Joash
Amaziah
Uzziah
Jotham
Ahaz

Hezekiah
Manasseh
Amon
Josiah
Jehoiakim
Jeconiah

Shealtiel
Zerubbabel
Abiud
Eliakim
Azor
Sadoc

Achim
Eliud
Eleazar
Matthan
Jacob
Joseph

Homework

Read the following two articles on Noah's Descendants and Race by bible-truth.org and the Origin of Race by Cooper P. Abrams, III

THE DESCENDANTS OF NOAH - Genesis Ten

https://bible-truth.org/GEN10.HTM

The Origin Of Race - By Cooper P. Abrams

https://idoc.pub/documents/the-origin-of-race-by-cooper-p-abrams-iii-5143x6g8pg4j

LESSON # 6: ABRAHAM'S BOSOM AND HADES

Over the last several weeks, we studied Lucifer. We learned that he was created the chief angel. He became proud and rebellious and was kicked out of heaven, and a third of the angels went with him. Today, we will find out where he went and what will happen to him in the future.

Where Did Lucifer/Satan Go After He Was Kicked Out Of Heaven?

Job 1:7 (NASB 1995)—*The LORD said to Satan, "From where do you come?" Then Satan answered the LORD and said, "From roaming about on the earth and walking around on it."*

1 Peter 5:8 (NASB 1995)—*Be of sober spirit, be on the alert. Your adversary, the devil, prowls around like a roaring lion, seeking someone to devour.*

Isaiah 14:11(NASB 1995)—*Your pomp and the music of your harps have been brought down to Sheol.* (prophetic of his future)

After Lucifer was cast out of the 3rd Heaven, he lost his name and his home. He is now referred to as Satan, Devil, Day Star (fallen angel), son of the morning, the anointed cherub, Beelzebub, Apollyon, Abaddon, Belial, Old Serpent, Dragon, Leviathan, Evil one, and many more.

What And Where Is Sheol?

Sheol/Hades

- In the **Old Testament Hebrew** Scriptures, the word used to describe the realm of the dead is **Sheol**. It simply means the "**place of the dead**" or the "**place of departed souls/spirits**."
- The **New Testament Greek word** used for hell is "**Hades**," which also refers to "**the place of the dead**." Other Scriptures in the New Testament indicate that

Sheol/Hades **is a temporary place, where souls are kept as they await the final resurrection and judgment.**

The Rich Man And Lazarus

Luke 16:19-31 (NASB 1995)—*"Now there was a rich man, and he habitually dressed in purple and fine linen, joyously living in splendor every day. "And a poor man named Lazarus was laid at his gate, covered with sores, and longing to be fed with the crumbs which were falling from the rich man's table; besides, even the dogs were coming and licking his sores. "Now the poor man died and was carried away by the angels to Abraham's bosom; and the rich man also died and was buried. "In Hades he lifted up his eyes, being in torment, and saw Abraham far away and Lazarus in his bosom. "And he cried out and said, 'Father Abraham, have mercy on me, and send Lazarus so that he may dip the tip of his finger in water and cool off my tongue, for I am in agony in this flame.' "But Abraham said, 'Child, remember that during your life you received your good things, and likewise Lazarus bad things; but now he is being comforted here, and you are in agony. 'And besides all this, between us and you there is a great chasm fixed, so that those who wish to come over from here to you will not be able, and that none may cross over from there to us.' "And he said, 'Then I beg you, father, that you send him to my father's house—for I have five brothers—in order that he may warn them, so that they will not also come to this place of torment.' "But Abraham said, 'They have Moses and the Prophets; let them hear them.' "But he said, 'No, father Abraham, but if someone goes to them from the dead, they will repent!' "But he said to him, 'If they do not listen to Moses and the Prophets, they will not be persuaded even if someone rises from the dead.'"*

Definitions

- **Sheol/Hades**—A realm with two divisions (*Matthew 11:23, 16:18; Luke 10:15, 16:23; Acts 2:27-31),* the abodes of the saved and the lost.
- **Abraham's Bosom**—The abode of the saved was called "paradise" and "Abraham's bosom."
  - The abodes of the saved and the lost are separated by a "great chasm" *(Luke 16:26).*
  - This is where Catholicism gets the belief that people go to purgatory when they die and are punished for their sins, and their loved ones pray them into heaven.

- When Jesus ascended to heaven, He took the occupants of paradise (believers) with Him *(Ephesians 4:8-10)*.
- When (a born again Christian) we die we will go directly up to Heaven. *(2 Corinthians 5:8)*

- **Hades**—The lost side of Sheol/Hades has remained unchanged. **All unbelieving dead go there awaiting their final judgment in the future**.
  - Did Jesus go to Sheol/Hades? Yes, according to Ephesians 4:8-10 and 1 Peter 3:18-20.
- **Sheol/Hades Location**—In the Greek (N.T) it meant primeval **deep**. In later Judaism it included the **interior depths of the earth** (*center*) and the **prison of evil spirits**.

Lake Of Fire

Lake of Fire (Hell) is the permanent and final place of judgment.

Revelation 19:20 (KJV)—*And the **beast** was taken, and with him the false prophet that wrought miracles before him, with which he deceived them that had received the mark of the beast, and them that worshipped his image. These both were cast alive into a lake of fire burning with brimstone.*

Revelation 20:10 (KJV)—*And the devil that deceived them was cast into the lake of fire and brimstone, where the beast and the false prophet are, and shall be tormented day and night for ever and ever.*

Revelation 20:14 (KJV)—*And death and hell (Hades) were cast into the lake of fire. This is the second death.*

Revelation 20:15 (KJV)—*And whosoever was not found written in the book of life was cast into the lake of fire.*

- After the great white throne judgment

Who Will Go To (Lake Of Fire/Hell)?

I Corinthians 6:9-11 (NASB 1995)—*Or do you not know that the unrighteous will not inherit the kingdom of God? Do not be deceived; neither fornicators, nor idolaters, nor adulterers, nor effeminate, nor homosexuals, nor thieves, nor the covetous, nor drunkards, nor revilers, nor swindlers, will inherit the kingdom of God. Such were some of you; but you were washed, but you were sanctified, but you were justified in the name of the Lord Jesus Christ and in the Spirit of our God.*

Revelation 21:8 (NASB 1995)—*But the fearful, and unbelieving, and the abominable, and murderers, and whoremongers, and sorcerers, and idolaters, and all liars, shall have their part in the lake which burneth with fire and brimstone: which is the second death.*

What Is The Lake Of Fire Like?

Revelation 20:10 (KJV)—*And the devil that deceived them was cast into the lake of fire and brimstone, where the beast and the false prophet are, and shall be tormented day and night for ever and ever.*

Matthew 13: 41-42 (NASB 1995)—*"The Son of Man will send forth His angels, and they will gather out of His kingdom all stumbling blocks, and those who commit lawlessness, and will throw them into the furnace of fire; in that place there will be weeping and gnashing of teeth.*

Matthew 8:12 (NASB 1995)—*"...but the sons of the kingdom will be cast out into the outer darkness; in that place there will be weeping and gnashing of teeth."*

2 Thessalonians 1:9 (NASB 1995)—*These will pay the penalty of eternal destruction, away from the presence of the Lord and from the glory of His power.*

Luke 16:24 (NASB 1995)—*"And he cried out and said, 'Father Abraham, have mercy on me, and send Lazarus so that he may dip the tip of his finger in water and cool off my tongue, for I am in agony in this flame.'"* (That is in Hades)

When Will Hades Become The Lake Of Fire?

"Hell" is in the future realm, only put into effect after the Great White Throne Judgment

Acts 17:30-31 (NASB 1995)—*"Therefore having overlooked the times of ignorance, God is now declaring to men that all people everywhere should repent, 31) because He has fixed a day in which He will judge the world in righteousness through a Man whom He has appointed, having furnished proof to all men by raising Him from the dead."*

Revelations 20:11-15 (NASB 1995)—(Judgment at the Throne of God) *Then I saw a great white throne and Him who sat upon it, from whose presence earth and heaven fled away, and no place was found for them. And I saw the dead, the great and the small, standing before the throne, and books were opened; and another book was opened, which is the book of life; and the dead were judged from the things which were written in the books, according to their deeds. And the sea gave up the dead which were in it, and death and Hades gave up the dead which were* *in them; and they were judged, every one of them according to their deeds. Then death and Hades were thrown into the lake of fire. This is the second death, the lake of fire. And if* anyone's name was not found written in the book of life, *he was thrown into the lake of fire.*

How Can I Stop Myself From Going To Hell?

Romans 3:23 (NASB 1995)—*For all have sinned, and come short of the glory of God.*

John 14:6 (NASB 1995)—*Jesus said to him, "I am the way, and the truth, and the life; no one comes to the Father but through Me.*

John 3:3 (KJV)—*Jesus answered and said unto him, Verily, verily, I say unto thee, Except a man be born again, he cannot see the kingdom of God.*

John 3:16 (NASB 1995)—*"For God so loved the world, that He gave His only begotten Son, that whoever believes in Him shall not perish, but have eternal life."*

Abraham's Bosom/Paradise

Before Christ's death and Resurrection, believers in the promise went to a place called Paradise or Abraham's Bosom.

Luke 23:43 (NASB 1995)—*And He said to him, "Truly I say to you, today you shall be with Me in Paradise."*

- *Pre-resurrection - Abraham's Bosom*)

I Peter 3:18-19 (KJV)—*For Christ also hath once suffered for sins, the just for the unjust, that he might bring us to God, being put to death in the flesh, but quickened by the Spirit:* 19 *By which also he went and preached unto the spirits in prison* (in Paradise)

- He preached the good news to those in Paradise

Rev. 1:17-19 (NASB 1995)—*When I saw Him, I fell at His feet like a dead man. And He placed His right hand on me, saying, "Do not be afraid; I am the first and the last, and the living One; and I was dead, and behold, I am alive forevermore, and I have the keys of death and of Hades. Therefore write the things which you have seen, and the things which are, and the things which will take place after these things.*

- He took the keys of death and Hell

Ephesians 4:7-10 (NASB 1995)—*But to each one of us grace was given according to the measure of Christ's gift. Therefore it says, "WHEN HE ASCENDED ON HIGH, HE LED CAPTIVE A HOST OF CAPTIVES, AND HE GAVE GIFTS TO MEN." (Now this expression, "He ascended," what does it mean except that He also had descended into the lower parts of the earth? He who descended is Himself also He who ascended far above all the heavens, so that He might fill all things.)*

- Paradise is **emptied** and those who were there ascended to Heaven with Jesus **leaving only Sheol/ Hades to house lost souls.**

What Happens To Believers When They Die Today (After Christ)?

Luke 16:22 (NASB 1995)—*"Now the poor man died and was carried away by the angels to Abraham's bosom; and the rich man also died and was buried."*

- Escorted by angels to heaven (soul/spirit)
- Body buried

II Cor. 5:6-10 (KJV)—*Therefore we are always confident, knowing that, whilst we are at home in the body, we are absent from the Lord: (For we walk by faith, not by sight:) We are confident, I say, and willing rather to be absent from the body, and to be present with the Lord.*

- This is your proof text

I Cor 15:41-44 (NASB 1995)—*There are also heavenly bodies and earthly bodies, but the glory of the heavenly is one, and the glory of the earthly is another. There is one glory of the sun, and another glory of the moon, and another glory of the stars; for star differs from star in glory. So also is the resurrection of the dead. It is sown a perishable body, it is raised an imperishable body; it is sown in dishonor, it is raised in glory; it is sown in weakness, it is raised in power; it is sown a natural body, it is raised a spiritual body. If there is a natural body, there is also a spiritual* body.

- Receive a heavenly body

Resurrected Bodies

Luke 24:36-43 (NASB 1995)—*While they were telling these things, He Himself stood in their midst and said to them, "Peace be to you." But they were startled and frightened and thought that they were seeing a spirit. And He said to them, "Why are you troubled, and why do doubts arise in your hearts? "See My hands and My feet, that it is I Myself; touch Me and see, for a spirit does not have flesh* *and bones as you see that I have." And when He had said this, He showed them His hands and His feet. While they still could not believe it because of their joy and amazement, He said to them, "Have you anything here to eat?" They gave Him a piece of a broiled fish; and He took it and ate it before them.*

- Jesus had a resurrected body
- He also ate.

I Cor. 15:50-52 (NASB 1995)—*Now I say this, brethren, that flesh and blood cannot inherit the kingdom of God; nor does the perishable inherit the imperishable. Behold, I tell you a mystery; we shall not all sleep, but we shall all be changed, in a moment, in the twinkling of an eye, at the last trumpet; for the trumpet will sound, and the dead will be raised imperishable, and we shall be changed.*

- Our bodies cannot enter heaven
- New heavenly body

Rev. 20:5-6 (NASB 1995)—*The rest of the dead did not come to life until the thousand years were completed. This is the first resurrection. Blessed and holy is the one who has a part in the first resurrection; over these the second death has no power, but they will be priests of God and of Christ, and will reign with Him for a thousand years.*

John 5:24-29 (NASB)—*"Truly, truly, I say to you, the one who hears My word, and believes Him who sent Me, has eternal life, and does not come into judgment, but has passed out of death into life. Truly, truly, I say to you, a time is coming and even now has arrived, when the dead will hear the voice of the Son of God, and those who hear will live. For just as the Father has life in Himself, so He gave to the Son also to have life in Himself; and He gave Him authority to execute judgment, because He is the Son of Man. Do not be amazed at this; for a time is coming when all who are in the tombs will hear His voice, and will come out: those who did the good deeds to a resurrection of life, those who committed the bad deeds to a resurrection of judgment."*

I Cor. 15:22-26 (NASB)—*For as in Adam all die, so also in Christ all will be made alive. But each in his own order: Christ the first fruits, after that those who are Christ's at His coming, then comes the end, when He hands over the kingdom to our God and Father, when He has abolished all rule and all authority and power. For He must reign until He has put all His enemies under His feet. The last enemy that will be abolished is death.*

I Cor. 15:50-57 (NASB)—*Now I say this, brothers and sisters, that flesh and blood cannot inherit the kingdom of God; nor does the perishable inherit the* *imperishable. Behold, I am telling you a mystery; we will not all sleep, but we will all be changed, in a moment, in the twinkling of an eye, at the last trumpet; for the trumpet will sound, and the dead will be raised imperishable, and we will be changed. For this perishable must put on the imperishable, and this mortal must put on immortality. But when this perishable puts on the imperishable, and this mortal puts on immortality, then will come about the saying that is written: "Death has been swallowed up in victory. Where, O Death, is your victory? Where, O Death, is your sting?" The sting of death is sin, and the power of sin is the Law; but thanks be to God, who gives us the victory through our Lord Jesus Christ.*

Philipians 3:20-21 (NASB)—*For our citizenship is in heaven, from which we also eagerly wait for a Savior, the Lord Jesus Christ; who will transform the body of our lowly condition into conformity with [m]His glorious body, by the exertion of the power that He has even to subject all things to Himself.*

- We will get a new body.

Soul Sleep

Some believe that when we die, our bodies are asleep in the grave until Jesus returns. The false doctrine of "soul sleep" teaches that, upon death, the soul of each person, believer and unbeliever alike, "sleeps" until the general resurrection.

- This doctrine is still taught as doctrine number 26 of the Seventh Day Adventist's 28 fundamental beliefs publication.
- It is also taught as the doctrine of the condition of the dead by Jehovah's Witnesses.
- Some Christian denominations adopted this belief too.
- This is why people go to the graves and speak to those who are "asleep".

What Will Heaven Be Like?

Rev. 21:1-4 (NASB)—*Then I saw a new heaven and a new earth; for the first heaven and the first earth passed away, and there is no longer any sea. And I saw the holy city, new Jerusalem, coming down out of heaven from God, prepared as a bride adorned for her husband. And I heard a loud voice from the throne, saying, "Behold, the tabernacle of God is among the people, and He will dwell among them, and they shall be His people, and God Himself will be among them, and He will wipe away every tear from their eyes; and there will no longer be any death;*

there will no longer be any mourning, or crying, or pain; the first things have passed away."

- God Himself will wipe away every tear from their eyes, and there shall no longer be death, mourning, or pain.

Rev. 22:1 (NASB)—*And he showed me a river of the water of life, clear as crystal, coming from the throne of God and of the Lamb,*

- Great river of the water of life (healing)

Rev. 22:3 (NASB)—*There will no longer be any curse; and the throne of God and of the Lamb will be in it, and His bond-servants will serve Him;*

- No longer be any curses

Rev. 22:5 (NASB)—*And there will no longer be any night; and they will not have need of the light of a lamp nor the light of the sun, because the Lord God will illuminate them; and they will reign forever and ever.*

- No night

We Do NOT Become Angels

Psalm 8:4-5 (KJV)—*What is man, that thou art mindful of him? and the son of man, that thou visitest him? For thou hast made him a little lower than the angels, and hast crowned him with glory and honour.*

- (angels)Hebrew word Elohim—a name for God
- Man was made a little lower than God, not angels.

Much of the angel literature refers to "the angel within". But angels are a separate part of the creation. They were created before man as a different kind. They are not within us. Notwithstanding the movie "It's a Wonderful Life" when we hear a bell ring it does not mean that an angel is getting his wings. Nor do good people, especially children, become angels when they die. We remain human beings—not angels, and certainly not God.

Who Will Go To Heaven?

Rev. 21:27 (NASB)—*and nothing unclean, and no one who practices abomination and lying, shall ever come into it, but only those whose names are written in the Lamb's book of life.*

- **Only those** whose names are written in the Lamb's book of life

Can A Name Be Taken Out Of The Book Once It Is Written?

Exodus 32:32-33 (KJV)—*Yet now, if thou wilt forgive their sin; and if not, blot me, I pray thee, out of thy book which thou hast written. And the LORD said unto Moses, Whosoever hath sinned against me, him will I blot out of my book.*

- The Israelites turned to other gods

Psalm 69:28 (KJV)—*Let them be blotted out of the book of the living, and not be written with the righteous.*

Blot Examples:

- Spilling liquid (water) on carpet and take a rag and blot out the water.
- Painting or pictures of inkblots or paint splatter

Meaning of blot:

- to make blots on; spot, stain, or blur
- to stain (a reputation); disgrace
- to erase or get rid of: memories *blotted* from one's mind
- to dry by soaking up the wet liquid, as with blotting paper

Daniel 12:1 (KJV)—*And at that time shall Michael stand up, the great prince which standeth for the children of thy people: and there shall be a time of trouble, such as never was since there was a nation even to that same time: and at that time thy people shall be delivered, every one that shall be found written in the book.*

- *End times*

Malachi 3:16 (KJV)—*Then they that feared the LORD spake often one to another: and the LORD hearkened, and heard it, and a book of remembrance was written before him for them that feared the LORD, and that thought upon his name.*

- Book of Remembrance

Rev. 3:5 (KJV)—*He that overcometh, the same shall be clothed in white raiment; and I will not blot out his name out of the book of life, but I will confess his name before my Father, and before his angels.*

- *End Times*

Those Who Won't Enter Heaven

Rev. 21:8 (NASB 1995)—*But for the cowardly and unbelieving and abominable and murderers and immoral persons and sorcerers and idolaters and all liars, their part will be in the lake that burns with fire and brimstone which is the second death.*

Rev. 20: 15 (NASB 1995)—*And if anyone's name was not found written in the book of life, he was thrown into the lake of fire.*

Object Lesson:

The Book of life—Use a large book (an old phone book would be perfect), tape the name "Lambs Book of Life" on the cover. Place the class attendance sheet in the book and at the end of class read all of the students' names. Show them what it will be like when they pass on from this earth, they will either be in the book of life or not. Explaining that when they accept Christ as their savior that their names are written in the Lambs book of life. If they turn from Him and worship other gods that it can be blotted out.

Only One Way to Heaven

John 14: 1-6 (NASB 1995)—*"Do not let your heart be troubled; believe in God, believe also in Me. "In My Father's house are many dwelling places; if it were not so, I would have told you; for I go to prepare a place for you. "If I go and prepare a place for you, I will come again and receive you to Myself, that where I am, there you may be also. "And you know the way where I am going." Thomas said to Him, "Lord, we do not know where You are going, how do we know the way?" Jesus said to him, "I am the way, and the truth, and the life; no one comes to the Father but through Me."*

- A place is being prepared
- "…but through me."

John 3:16-21 (NASB 1995)—*"For God so loved the world, that He gave His only begotten Son, that whoever believes in Him shall not perish, but have eternal life. "For God did not send the Son into the world to judge the world, but that the world might be saved through Him. "He who believes in Him is not judged; he who does not believe has been judged already, because he has not believed in the name of the only begotten Son of God. "This is the judgment, that the Light has come into the world, and men loved the darkness rather than the Light, for their deeds were evil. "For everyone who does evil hates the Light, and does not come to the Light* *for fear that his deeds will be exposed. "But he who practices the truth comes to the Light, so that his deeds may be manifested as having been wrought in God."*

- The Plan of God for salvation
- **We are eternal beings**—you will live forever whether that is Heaven or Hell that is up to you!

Question: Is your name written in the Lamb's Book of Life?

LESSON # 7: WHAT THE BIBLE TELLS US ABOUT ANGELS

Angels Are Ministering Spirits Assigned To Us By God

Hebrews 1:14 (KJV)—*Are they not all ministering spirits, sent forth to minister for them who shall be heirs of salvation?*

- They are to minister both to us and for us

Warnings!

Duet. 4:19 (NASB 1995)—*And beware not to lift up your eyes to heaven and see the sun and the moon and the stars, all the host of heaven, and be drawn away and worship them and serve them, those which the LORD your God has allotted to all the peoples under the whole heaven.*

- Example: Tower of Babel
- **Do not be intrigued by or entertained by angels**. God warned us to never worship angels.
- **Remember Lucifer's original sin?** He wanted to be worshipped. He is still trying to deceive people into worshipping him!
- Angel encounters/stories are always fascinating but can lead to deception.
    - Remember that 1/3 of the angels rebelled along with Satan. These are known as fallen angels and also called evil ones. The Bible will refer to them as demons.
    - Fallen angels/demons can disguise themselves as good angels or ministers of light. These fallen angels have deceived many people in our culture who have embraced "angel mania." *(More on that later.)*
    - **The only acknowledgment** of angels should be of their presence and power!

Ranking

- Cherubs
- Guardian angels
- Archangels

Only Three Angels Are Named In The Bible

- **Michael**—protector of Israel
- **Gabriel**—proclaimer of the Lord
- **Lucifer**—Son of the morning and worshipper

If someone refers to an angel by name that is not in the Bible, they are most likely being entertained/deceived by a **demon** and they don't know it.

Role or Descriptions

- Angels are all around us
- Excel in strength and are Powerful
- Different levels or rankings
- Enforce the Word of God
- Words activate them or give them assignments
- Will not forgive nor hold a grudge (They are not human – Exodus 23:20-21)
- Are the muscles of heaven
- Very intelligent
- Not limited to time or space
- Messengers **NOT** teachers
- Put to work by the words of our mouth
- Supernatural
- Minister to and for God's people

Words Activate Them Or Give Them Assignments

> **Psalms 103:20** (KJV)—*Bless the LORD, ye His angels, that excel in strength, that do His commandments, hearkening unto the voice of His word.*

- Excel in Strength
- **Do His commandments**—not the 10 commandments *(What God speaks for them to do, how do you know what God speaks to them?*)
- **Hearkening** to the **voice of His Word.**
- No examples in the Bible of angels hearkening to "your" voice. *Their job is to perform God's Word & His will.*

Psalms 91:11 (NASB 1995)—*For He will give His angels charge concerning you, to guard you in all your ways.*

- Watch the words that come out of your mouth! Our words activate our angels**.** If we don't speak the Word they have nothing to give "heed" to. Remember, they only give heed to the Word of God only!
- When you are in dire circumstances and you fill your mouth with the Word of God, it activates them to your service.
- Watch that you don't speak out against God, His will or His Word!

Object Lesson:

Hearkening to the voice of His Word (Bible). Hold up the Bible to a microphone (nothing happens). When I give voice to this Bible; say what it says or pray the Word, the angels hearken unto the voice of the Word of God. We must give voice to the word!

Examples Of Angels Hearkening To The Voice Of His Word

Matthew 4:1-4 (NASB 1995)—*Then Jesus was led up by the Spirit into the wilderness to be tempted by the devil. And after He had fasted forty days and forty nights, He then became hungry. And the tempter came and said to Him, "If You are the Son of God, command that these stones become bread." But He answered and said, "It is written, 'MAN SHALL NOT LIVE ON BREAD ALONE, BUT ON EVERY WORD THAT PROCEEDS OUT OF THE MOUTH OF GOD.'"*

- Jesus Overcame Satan by the voice of the Word of God during a great battle

Matthew 4:11 (NASB 1995) *Then the devil left Him; and behold, angels came and began to minister to Him.*

- After he was tempted, the angels came and ministered to him (his physical body). When we are frail in our body, they give strength to us.
- Another Example: Elijah (I Kings 19) – angels came and woke him up and fed him, strengthened him for 40 days.

- In both of these examples angels actually fed Jesus and Elijah that provided strength for the natural bodies.

There was a great famine in the land of Israel. The Prophet Elisha gets up and says, tomorrow at this time we will have barley and flour, and it will be sold for such and such.

Angel Armies

2 Kings 6:8-23 (NASB 1995)—*Now the king of Aram was warring against Israel; and he counseled with his servants saying, "In such and such a place shall be my camp." The man of God sent word to the king of Israel saying, "Beware that you do not pass this place, for the Arameans are coming down there." The king of Israel sent to the place about which the man of God had told him; thus he warned him, so that he guarded himself there, more than once or twice. Now the heart of the king of Aram was enraged over this thing; and he called his servants and said to them, "Will you tell me which of us is for the king of Israel?" One of his servants said, "No, my lord, O king; but Elisha, the prophet who is in Israel, tells the king of Israel the words that you speak in your bedroom." So he said, "Go and see where he is, that I may send and take him." And it was told him, saying, "Behold, he is in Dothan." He sent horses and chariots and a great army there, and they came by night and surrounded the city. Now when the attendant of the man of God had risen early and gone out, behold, an army with horses and chariots was circling the city. And his servant said to him, "Alas, my master! What shall we do?" So he answered, "Do not fear, for those who are with us are more than those who are with them." Then Elisha prayed and said, "O Lord, I pray, open his eyes that he may see." And the Lord opened the servant's eyes and he saw; and behold, the mountain was full of horses and chariots of fire all around Elisha. When they came down to him, Elisha prayed to the Lord and said, "Strike this people with blindness, I pray." So He struck them with blindness according to the word of Elisha. Then Elisha said to them, "This is not the way, nor is this the city; follow me and I will bring you to the man whom you seek." And he brought them to Samaria. When they had come into Samaria, Elisha said, "O Lord, open the eyes of these men, that they may see." So the Lord opened their eyes and they saw; and behold, they were in the midst of Samaria. Then the king of Israel when he saw them, said to Elisha, "My father, shall I kill them? Shall I kill them?" He answered, "You shall not kill them. Would you kill those you have taken captive with your sword and with your bow? Set bread and water before them, that they may eat and drink and go to their master." So he prepared a great feast for them; and when they had eaten and drunk he sent them away, and they went to their* *master. And the marauding bands of Arameans did not come again into the land of Israel.*

- Holy Spirit speaks thru Elisha (prophets in the OT)
- Angels around us

Elisha Promises Food

2 Kings 7:1-20 (NASB 1995)—*Then Elisha* (prophet) *said, "Listen to the word of the LORD; thus says the LORD, 'Tomorrow about this time a measure of fine flour will be sold for a shekel, and two measures of barley for a shekel, in the gate of Samaria." The royal officer on whose hand the king was leaning answered the man of God and said, "Behold, if the LORD should make windows in heaven, could this thing be?"* (He mocked or despised the word of the prophet and spoke contrary/against) *Then he said, "Behold, you will see it with your own eyes, but you will not eat of it." Now there were four leprous men at the entrance of the gate; and they said to one another, "Why do we sit here until we die?*

Leprosy was a disease that ate away the skin. It was highly contagious and caused severe disfigurement (ete away the limbs, ears, nose, and flesh). People with leprosy were shunned or banned and sent away to tombs to live together.

If we say, 'We will enter the city,' then the famine is in the city and we will die there; and if we sit here, we die also. Now therefore come, and let us go over to the camp of the Arameans. If they spare us, we will live; and if they kill us, we will but die." They arose at twilight to go to the camp of the Arameans; when they came to the outskirts of the camp of the Arameans, behold, there was no one there. For the Lord had caused the army of the Arameans to hear a ***sound of chariots and a sound of horses****, (host of heaven/angels) even the sound of a* ***great army****, so that they said to one another, "Behold, the king of Israel has hired against us the kings of the Hittites and the kings of the Egyptians, to come upon us." Therefore they arose and fled in the twilight, and left their tents and their horses and their donkeys, even the camp just as it was, and fled for their life. When these lepers came to the outskirts of the camp, they entered one tent and ate and drank, and carried from there silver and gold and clothes, and went and hid them; and they returned and entered another tent and carried from there also, and went and hid them.*

Then they said to one another, "We are not doing right. This day is a day of good news, but we are keeping silent; if we wait until morning light, punishment will overtake us. **(They thought that they would somehow be punished for keeping it to themselves)** *Now therefore come, let us go and tell the king's household."*

So they came and called to the gatekeepers of the city, and they told them, saying, "We came to the camp of the Arameans, and behold, there was no one there, nor the voice of man, only the horses tied and the donkeys tied, and the tents just as they were." The gatekeepers called and told it within the king's household. Then the king arose in the night and said to his servants, "I will now tell you what the Arameans have done to us. They know that we are hungry; therefore they have gone from the camp to hide themselves in the field, saying, 'When they come out of the city, we will capture them alive and get into the city.'" One of his servants said, "Please, let some men take five of the horses which remain, which are left in the city. Behold, they will be in any case like all the multitude of Israel who are left in it; behold, they will be in any case like all the multitude of Israel who have already perished, so let us send and see." They took therefore two chariots with horses, and the king sent after the army of the Arameans, saying, "Go and see."

The Promise Fulfilled

They went after them to the Jordan, and behold, all the way was full of clothes and equipment which the Arameans had thrown away in their haste. Then the messengers returned and told the king.

So the people went out and plundered the camp of the Arameans. Then a measure of fine flour was sold for a shekel and two measures of barley for a shekel, according to the word of the LORD. Now the king appointed the royal officer on whose hand he leaned to have charge of the gate; but the people trampled on him at the gate, and he died just as the man of God had said, who spoke when the king came down to him. It happened just as the man of God had spoken to the king, saying, "Two measures of barley for a shekel and a measure of fine flour for a shekel, will be sold tomorrow about this time at the gate of Samaria." Then the royal officer answered the man of God and said, "Now behold, if the LORD should make windows in heaven, could such a thing be?" And he said, "Behold, you will see it with your own eyes, but you will not eat of it." And so it happened to him, for the people trampled on him at the gate and he died.

- The royal officer spoke contrary to the Word of God

The Red Sea

Exodus 14: 15-19 (NASB 1995)—*Then the LORD said to Moses, "Why are you crying out to Me? Tell the sons of Israel to go forward. "As for you, lift up your staff and stretch out your hand over the sea and divide it, and the sons of Israel* *shall go through the midst of the sea on dry land. "As for Me, behold, I will harden the hearts of the Egyptians so that they will go in after them; and I will be honored through Pharaoh and all his army, through his chariots and his horsemen. "Then the Egyptians will know that I am the LORD, when I am honored through Pharaoh, through his chariots and his horsemen."*

The angel of God, who had been going before the camp of Israel, moved and went behind them; and the pillar of cloud moved from before them and stood behind them.

- At the Red sea, mountain beside them, sea in front and the enemy behind him. All insurmountable!
- **Speak** and **lift up your rod, stretch out the sea and speak to it**.
- The angel of God went from going before them and went behind them.
- The pillar cloud moved and went behind them.
- The **angel had power over the cloud** to protect Israel and be a light to the Jews. This one angel had a lot of power. (One angel for 2 ½ million people)

Apostles Jailed

Acts 5:17 (1995 NASB)—*But the high priest rose up, along with all his associates (that is the sect of the Sadducees), and they were filled with jealousy. They laid hands on the apostles and put them in a public jail. "Go, stand and speak to the people in the temple the whole message of this Life."*

- The high priest rose up and put the apostle in prison
- **God sent an angel** to get them out of prison.
- Go and stand and speak to the people.

Peter Jailed

Acts 12 1-10 (NASB 1995)—*Now about that time Herod the king laid hands on some who belonged to the church in order to mistreat them. And he had James the brother of John put to death with a sword. When he saw that it pleased the Jews, he proceeded to arrest Peter also. Now it was during the days of Unleavened Bread. When he had seized him, he put him in prison, delivering him to four squads of soldiers to guard him, intending after the Passover to bring him out before the people. So Peter was kept in the prison, but prayer for him was being made fervently by the church to God.*

On the very night when Herod was about to bring him forward, Peter was sleeping between two soldiers, bound with two chains, and guards in front of the door were watching over the prison. And behold, an angel of the Lord suddenly appeared and a light shone in the cell; and he struck Peter's side and woke him up, saying, "Get up quickly." And his chains fell off his hands. And the angel said to him, "Gird yourself and put on your sandals." And he did so. And he said to him, "Wrap your cloak around you and follow me." And he went out and continued to follow, and he did not know that what was being done by the angel was real, but thought he was seeing a vision. When they had passed the first and second guard, they came to the iron gate that leads into the city, which opened for them by itself; and they went out and went along one street, and immediately the angel departed from him.

- Herod killed James and tried to take Peter
- **Prayer was made** without ceasing and behold, an angel of the Lord came and touched Peter.
- Thick chains and locks fell off. Gird yourself and put your shoes and clothes on.
- The iron gate opened of its own accord. They went out one street, and the angel left him.

Angels Can Be Provoked

Lot And His Family

Genesis 19:15-26 (NASB 1995)—*When morning dawned, the angels urged Lot, saying, "Up, take your wife and your two daughters who are here, or you will be swept away in the punishment of the city." But he hesitated. So, the men seized his hand and the hand of his wife and the hands of his two daughters, for the <u>compassion of the LORD was upon him</u>; and they brought him out, and put him outside the city. When they had brought them outside, one said, "Escape for your life! Do not look behind you, and do not stay anywhere in the valley; escape to the mountains, or you will be swept away." But Lot said to them, "Oh no, my lords! Now behold, your servant has found favor in your sight, and you have magnified your lovingkindness, which you have shown me by saving my life; but I cannot escape to the mountains, for the disaster will overtake me and I will die; now behold, this town is near enough to flee to, and it is small. Please, let me escape there (is it not small?) that my life may be saved." He said to him, "Behold, I grant you this request also, not to overthrow the town of which you have spoken. Hurry,* *escape there, for I cannot do anything until you arrive there." Therefore the name of the town was called Zoar.*

The sun had risen over the earth when Lot came to Zoar. Then the LORD rained on Sodom and Gomorrah brimstone and fire from the LORD out of heaven, and He overthrew those cities, and all the valley, and all the inhabitants of the cities, and what grew on the ground. But his wife, from behind him, looked back, and she became a pillar of salt.

Abraham intercedes for his nephew Lot and his family and God sends angels to rescue them. Lot's wife died because she provoked the angels God sent to deliver her.

Angels had to take Lots' hand, don't look back! They were given an assignment.

- **Don't provoke the angel**—they are not human. They don't have a soul or heart like we do. They have an assignment only! She provoked the angel.
- Prov. 23:20—He won't forgive you if you provoke him! She became a pillar of salt.
- Jesus referred to it in Luke 17:32, "remember Lot's wife". She **provoked the angel.**
- He's not going to wink at it; he's not going to forgive you.
- He tried to give her a way out, a way escape, and she did it anyway—act of rebellion and disobedience.
- **Accusations against God with unbelief can provoke** your angels, and it can go badly for you.
- Most people only see the good side of angels (sweet and puffy) but, angels excel in power and strength.
- Angels are not limited to time and space, very intelligent, put to work by the words that come out of your mouth.

Pharaoh

Exodus 23:20-22 (NASB 1995*)—"Behold, I am going to send an angel before you to guard you along the way and to bring you into the place which I have prepared. 21 "Be on your guard before him and obey his voice; do not be rebellious toward him, for he will not pardon your transgression, since My name is in him. 22 "But if you truly obey his voice and do all that I say, then I will be an enemy to your enemies and an adversary to your adversaries.*

- Pharaoh cursed God and His people (plagues were performed by God's angels, not demons)

Angel's Bring Messages

Angels Do Not Teach. When someone says an angel came and taught them something, it is a deceiving spirit / demon. Look at the various cults that started with "an angel from God" who taught/gave them a "new" doctrine contrary to the Word of God. (Jehovah's Witness, Mormons, Muslims etc.)

Zachariah And The Angel Gabriel

Luke 1:11-15 (NASB 1995)—*And an angel of the Lord appeared to him, standing to the right of the altar of incense. Zacharias was troubled when he saw the angel, and fear gripped him. But the angel said to him, "Do not be afraid, Zacharias, for your petition has been heard, and your wife Elizabeth will bear you a son, and you will give him the name John. "You will have joy and gladness, and many will rejoice at his birth. "For he will be great in the sight of the Lord; and he will drink no wine or liquor, and he will be filled with the Holy Spirit while yet in his mother's womb.*

- Zachariah saw an angel of the Lord (prayer is heard)
- Your Wife is going to have a baby, he is going to be great (*he should have said, "that's great!")*
- **Whereby shall I know this?** I am an old man (Full of doubt) - Angel says, I am Gabriel!
- Now you will be dumb.
- Why? Because of vs. 18 You didn't believe my Word. They have the power to cut your mouth off and fix your mouth to prevent you from destroying God's plan.

Mary

Luke 1:26 (NASB 1995)—*Now in the sixth month the angel Gabriel was sent from God to a city in Galilee called Nazareth, to a virgin engaged to a man whose name was Joseph, of the descendants of David; and the virgin's name was Mary. And coming in, he said to her, "Greetings, favored one! The Lord is with you." But she was very perplexed at this statement, and kept pondering what kind of salutation* *this was. The angel said to her, "Do not be afraid, Mary; for you have found favor with God. "And behold, you will conceive in your womb and bear a son, and you shall name Him Jesus. "He will be great and will be called the Son of the Most High; and the Lord God will give Him the throne of His father David; and He will reign over the house of Jacob forever, and His kingdom will have no end." Mary said to the angel, "How can this be, since I am a virgin?" The angel answered and said to her, "The Holy Spirit will come upon you, and the power of the Most High will overshadow you; and for that reason the holy Child shall be called the Son of God. "And behold, even your relative Elizabeth has also conceived a son in her old age; and she who was called barren is now in her sixth month. "For nothing will be impossible with God." And Mary said, "Behold, the bondslave of the Lord; may it be done to me according to your word." And the angel departed from her.*

- Troubled, but not doubtful of his saying.
- She questioned him, didn't doubt him. Just asking a legitimate question.
- Vs. 38 – **Be it unto me according to thy Word**! No doubting, nothing happened to her because the angel wasn't provoked.
- God was able to prepare a way before her, a place that He had prepared!
- **Look at the two different responses to the Word of God!**

The Deception of Evil, Fallen Angels

As the arch deceiver and antagonist to God, the church, and mankind as whole, Satan is the master of disguise. It is clearly his masquerade as an angel of light with his servant angels, who also disguise themselves in one way or another, that are behind the current Angel mania in our society today.

There are many books, publications, and seminars that are filled with demonic deception of the ugliest kind. **Because when you start talking to angels, you end up dealing with demons.**

Discerning The Activity Of These Demonic, Evil Angels

You know you're around "fallen angels" or demons masquerading as angels of light and holiness **when you see or hear these terms**:

Contacting Or Communing With Angels

- The Bible gives **neither permission nor precedent for contacting angels.**
- When people start **calling on angels**, it's **not the holy angels who answer**. They're demons, disguising themselves as good angels to people who don't know how to tell the difference.

Loving Our Angels, Praying To Our Angels

- Some self-styled "angel experts" instruct their followers to love their angels and call upon them for health, healing, prosperity, and guidance. But angels are God's servants, and all this attention and emphasis and glory should go to God, not His servants. God says, "I will not share my glory with another" (Isaiah 42:8).
- Scripture makes no mention of loving angels—only God, His word, and people. And it never tells us to pray to angels, only to the Lord Himself.

Instruction, Knowledge, Or Insight From Angels, Particularly Ones With Names

- Some angel teachers are proclaiming that angels are trying very hard to contact us, so they can give us deeper knowledge of the spiritual (Karyn Martin-Kuri, in an interview with *Body, Mind and Spirit* Journal, May/June 1993. Also, Albright, Naomi, *Angel Walk*, Tuscaloosa, Alabama: Portals Press, 1990). Invariably, this **"angel knowledge" is a mixture of truth and lies**, and never stands up to the absolute truth of Scripture.
- There are four angel names that keep popping up in the angel literature: Michael, Gabriel, Uriel, and Raphael. **Michael and Gabriel are the only angels mentioned by name in the Bible**. The other two show up in the apocryphal *First Book of Enoch*, which includes a fanciful account of the actions of these four beings.
- Those who **report modern-day angel teachings are actually channeling information from demons.**

Special Knowledge Or Teachings From Angels

- Naomi Albright distributes teachings about the deep meanings of colors, and numbers and letters of the alphabet which she claims is "knowledge given from above and brought forth in more detail by the High Angelic Master Sheate, Lady Master Cassandra, and Angel Carpelpous, and the Master Angel, One on High." (*Paths of Light* newsletter, Angel Walk F.O.L., Followers of Light, No. 24, July 1994, p. 6-10). These same beings told Mrs. Albright to stress two main teachings: **first, that God accepts all religions, and second, Reincarnation**.

(Albright, *Angel Walk*, p. 77-78). These two teachings keep showing up in much of the **New Age angel literature**, which shouldn't be surprising since they are heretical lies that come from the pit of hell, which is where the angel teachers are from.

- Other angel teachings are that **all is a part of God** (pantheism); the learner is set apart from others by the "deep" knowledge that the angels give (this is a basic draw to the occult); and that eventually, the one who pursues contact with these angels will be **visited by an Ascended Master or a Shining Angel** (*which is a personal encounter with a demon).*
- We need to remember that **God's angels are not teachers**. God's word says they are messengers—that's what "angel" means—and they minister to us. God has revealed to us everything we need for life and godliness (**2 Peter 1:3), so any hidden knowledge that spirit beings try to impart is by nature occultic and demonic.**
- Islam - Mohammad, Mormons - Joseph Smith, Jehovah's Witnesses – angel guides

Human Divinity

- The message of the ugly angels is that we need to recognize that **we are one with the divine, we are divine...we are God**. In Karen Goldman's *The Angel Book: A Handbook for Aspiring Angels*, she says things like, "Angels don't fall out of the sky; they emerge from within." (Goldman, Karen, *The Angel Book—A Handbook for Aspiring Angels*, New York: Simon & Shuster, 1988, p. 20). **And, "The whole purpose in life is to know your Angel Self, accept it and be it. In this way we finally experience true oneness**." (Ibid., p. 95).
- Much of the angel literature refers to **"the angel within**." But angels are a separate part of the creation. They were created before man as a different kind. **They are not *within us*.** The movie "It's a Wonderful Life" notwithstanding, when we hear a bell ring it does not mean that an angel is getting his wings. Nor do good people, especially children, become angels when they die. We remain human beings—not angels, and certainly not God.
- What our culture needs in response to the angel craze is strong discernment built on the foundation of God's word. We need to remember, and share with others, three truths about angels:
    - The ministry of holy angels will never contradict the Bible.
    - The actions of holy angels will always be consistent with the character of Christ.

- A genuine encounter with a holy angel will glorify God, not the angel. Holy angels never draw attention to themselves. They typically do their work and disappear.

Entertaining Angels Unaware

Hebrews 13:2 (NASB 1995)—*Do not neglect to show hospitality to strangers, for by this some have entertained angels without knowing it.*

- It's very true that many have "entertained angels unaware". But we need to make sure we're entertaining the right kind of angels!

Role Of The Holy Spirit And Angels In Our Lives

The Holy Spirit and Angels <u>don't</u> do the same things; they are different.

- Holy Spirit (inside)
  - God's spirit that lives inside of you
  - He is our Teacher—He leads you and guides you into all truth *(angels do not)*
  - He dwells **in you** and ministers to your soul and spirit *(angels minister to your body)*
  - He gives **you power** to stand against the enemy
  - The Holy Spirit lives <u>in you</u>
- Angels (outside)
  - Angels are the muscle of heaven! The enforcers.
  - **Proclaim**—(Are **messengers**) – proclaimer of what is **God has already established**
  - **Provide**—Comfort in the **natural in the realm – body**. His comfort inside of you in your soul and your spirit.
  - They minister for and to you and **prepare** the way for you *(move things, provide things)*
  - They **Protect** you!
  - Angels are all **around you**!

Homework

Read the article attached on angels and deception

https://bible.org/article/angels-god's-ministering-spirits

Suggested Reading For Those Wanting To Know More

Frank Peretti's "This Present Darkness"

Perry Stone's "Angels on Assignment

Angels on Assignment by Charles and Frances Hunter told by Roland Buck.

Jesse Duplantis' video clip on his experience with angels or anyone else legitimate (***that lines up with the Word)*** experience/testimony.

https://www.youtube.com/watch?v=Luw6cMuPLVc

BIOGRAPHY

A native of Wilmington, Delaware, Gwen Thornton now resides in Central Pennsylvania. She and her husband Philip Thornton are founding pastors at Legacy Faith Church in Harrisburg, Pennsylvania.

Mother to four children and grandmother to six, Ms. Thornton has taught Bible curriculum to students ranging from toddlers to adults. She writes her own curriculum because of the lack of high-quality faith-based materials available.

A perpetual student of the Bible, Ms. Thornton finds the intricate study of the Old and New Testaments and teachings of Jesus Christ the foundations upon which her life is based.

In answering her call to ministry, Pastor Gwen Thornton believes it is a collective responsibility to raise children and adults alike with a sound spiritual foundation for their daily life.

Knowing that salvation only comes by grace through faith, she understands the importance of teaching the message of faith.

She hopes that her detailed curricula will reach church schools of all denominations and inspire teachers to guide new believers to hear the Gospel of Jesus Christ in a Biblically-sound, fun, informative, and relatable manner.

www.ingramcontent.com/pod-product-compliance
Lightning Source LLC
Chambersburg PA
CBHW050503110426
42742CB00018B/3357
* 9 7 8 1 6 4 4 5 7 2 7 4 0 *